The Game is Up

Book 2

We believe that the Bible is God's word to mankind, and that it contains everything we need to know in order to be reconciled with God and live in a way that is pleasing to him. Therefore, we believe it is vital to teach children accurately from the Bible, being careful to teach each passage's true meaning in an appropriate way for childlren, rather than selecting a 'children's message' from a Biblical passage.

© TnT Ministries
29 Buxton Gardens, Acton, London, W3 9LE
Tel: +44 (0) 20 8992 0450 Fax: +44 (0) 20 8896 1847
email: sales@tntministries.org.uk

Contributors Trevor Blundell; Thalia Blundell; John & Carolyn Chamberlain; Annie Gemmill; Steve Johnson; Guy Lachlan; Nick Margesson; Leonie Mason; Kirsteen McCulloch; Kathy Pierce

Published in 2002 by Christian Focus Publications Ltd.
Geanies House, Fearn, Tain, Ross-shire, IV20 1TW
Tel: 01862 871 011 Fax: 01862 871 699
email: info@christianfocus.com

Cover design by Tim Charnick
Illustrations by Tim Charnick
Page 75 - illustrations by Tim Charnick from The Mission Zone published by Christian Focus Publications and Overseas Missionary Fellowship.
Printed by Arrowsmith

This book and other in the series can be purchased from your local Christian bookshop. Alternatively you can write to TnT Ministries direct or place your order with the publisher.

ISBN 1-85792-760-5

Contents

Introduction

The great desire of our hearts is that children everywhere will come to love and trust Jesus as their Lord and Saviour. It is our firm belief that this happens primarily through the teaching of God's word in the Bible. This book of games and ideas is designed as a resource to complement and support Bible teaching. It has been written as a companion volume to the 'On the Way' Bible teaching programme, but is suitable for use in any situation where the Bible is being taught to children.

Teaching the Bible is an exacting task. Teaching the Bible to children is even more so. The concepts are sometimes hard to communicate and are often contrary to the norms in the secular society in which they live. They are used to an interactive style of learning and they want to have fun. Traditionally we have tended to separate off the 'Bible teaching' slot from the rest of the activities in our children's programmes which are fun but have no Bible content. How much better to make every part of the programme count in the teaching of God's word! Since children learn by repetition, why teach something once when you can teach it several times, using all the activities and games to contribute to the learning process? In this way not only is learning enhanced but the Bible is exciting, relevant and truly central to the group's activities.

In this book we have outlined 3 supplementary activities - the Warm Up, the Consolidation and the Wind Up. Though this is only one model of an integrated teaching approach, it has been used by TnT Ministries with great success for many years. We have found consistently that with this kind of repetition even the smallest child can learn big things about God.

Warm Up

This is a short activity or presentation designed to arrest the attention of the children and prepare them for the Bible teaching which is to follow.

Consolidation

This is a constructive game or activity designed to reinforce the key concepts, theme, aim or details of the Bible story that has just been taught. It generally involves plenty of physical activity and some simple equipment.

Wind Up

A Wind Up is the final summation of the days teaching. It involves linking the Warm Up, the Bible story and the Consolidation together, emphasising the central teaching point.

Warm ups and wind ups take around 5 minutes and a Consolidation game 10-15 minutes. For each Bible story there are 2 schemes of Warm Ups, Consolidations and Wind Ups described. One will often require more space or more equipment.

The ideas and suggestions in this book are only guidelines for you to adapt and change in line with the age, number and needs of your children and limitations of your meeting space. We would stress that they should be used alongside, not in place of, teaching directly from the Bible.

In some warm ups the leader demonstrates negative qualities, such as favouritism. When acting out of character we suggest that you don a hat or jacket, or call yourself a different name, so that the younger children do not equate the bad points with the leader.

Creating your own Games

Why not create your own games, custom made to serve your children, and take advantage of the special possibilities of your meeting place? It's easy if you take account of a few basic principles.

The first task is to spend time in the Bible. Your game is a teaching opportunity and you need to understand the message of your passage for the day before you will know the concept, aim or details you want to teach from it via the game. There are four important elements to designing and running successful games.

Rules

There need to be SIMPLE RULES which are easily understood and which can be enforced to make the game fun, safe, workable and educational.

- Explain the rules, then ask questions to see if they have understood them. Then ask if they have any questions before repeating the rules and starting the game. This may sound laborious but it is a good investment of time.
- Start the game with a clear command, e.g. 'When I say GO', or, 'When I drop my hand'.
- The rules must be applied consistently and rule breakers need to be dealt with firmly.

Participation

Games are for joining in, not for watching, and so good games involve lots of participation. To make a game fun for everyone, as many children as possible need to be on the move at the same time. However, a safe environment must be preserved at all times.

- Games involving cross movements of children or games depending on speed alone are best avoided.
- Small or otherwise vulnerable children must be protected. Sometimes it is possible to design a game where these children have a different role from the older ones. All children should be encouraged to take part but never forced.
- It is wise to have a strategy for stopping the game and restoring order if necessary. The command 'Statues' or 'Freeze' will do this. A 'Sin Bin' is also useful for rule breakers.

A Scoring System

A scoring system is needed to determine who wins. Children are naturally competitive and learning to win and lose graciously is a valuable social skill. However:

- It must be absolutely fair and administered by an impartial adult.
- It must be understandable, preferably visual.
- All efforts should be affirmed and congratulated.

A running commentary by the game leader is very helpful.

Equipment

Equipment os some sort is needed for nearly all games. Children like to hold, carry and hide things.

- Almost anything can be used in games, but it must be safe. It is unwise to include anything which might be used as a weapon.
- It should be easy to reset if necessary during the game and easy to clear up at the end.
- The ideal is to have a small store of safe, versatile itmes for use in your games.

List of suggested items

Balloons & blow-up items	Empty plastic soft drink bottles	Sheet or parachute
Balls of string	Newspapers	Soft sponge balls
Buckets	Small items to act as tokens	Sponges
Cardboard boxes	e.g. bottle tops, corks, buttons	Table tennis balls
Cardboard tubes	Plastic jar lids	
Clothesline x 18m. lengths	Plastic laundry baskets or sledges	
Dried peas, beans, lentils, etc.		
Disposable or plastic cups	Puppets - 2 - one boy - one girl	

VICTORY PROMISED

Text: Read and study Judges 6:1-40.

Teaching point: God requires obedience from his followers.

WARM UP 1

Leader 1 starts to introduce the theme of God requiring obedience. He is interrupted by leader 2, who says that he thinks we should do another theme, such as God's love. Leader 2 starts expounding on God's love, but is interrupted by another leader, who proposes a third theme and starts expounding it. Any other leaders can interrupt with yet other themes. (If there are only 2 leaders present, leader 1 changes his mind and introduces a third theme, then leader 2 introduces a fourth theme.) An argument ensues. Leader 1 calls order and says that we cannot make progress with conflicting ideas. He must make the decision because he is in charge.

In today's true story from the Bible the Israelites had been listening to conflicting voices. They were listening to other gods, as well as to the true God. So God punished them. I want you to come back and tell me:

1. What was the name of the man God chose to deliver his people?

2. What did God tell him to do at night?

3. How did God show him that he was the right man for the job of deliverer?

CONSOLIDATION 1

The object is to show what it was like for the Israelites when they did not do things God's way. Mark out a safety zone at one end of the room. Some of the leaders stand, legs apart, facing away from the safety zone (see diagram). The children are the Israelites and act out the leader's commands, such as 'plant seed', 'hoe the ground', 'plough the land', 'rest break', etc. When the leader shouts, 'Midianites!' the children try to get to the safety zone by crawling through the leaders' legs. Other leaders try to catch them before they get to the safety zone. The catchers should be restricted in number (say 2) and confined to a middle area (see diagram). On 'Israelites' the children resume their duties as directed.

WIND UP 1

Remind the children of the Warm Up and how impossible it was when listening to conflicting voices. Review the questions from the Warm Up. God expects his people to do what he says, just like the Israelites in the game.

VICTORY PROMISED

Text: Read and study Judges 6:1-40.

Teaching point: The importance of trusting God.

WARM UP 2

Leader 1 is introduced by another leader as 'Mr Weak and Wobbly'. He is wearing a silly hat and/or other articles. He speaks words in the wrong order, stammers, is nervous and clumsy. He tells the children that he has been asked to step in for their usual leader today. He is not sure what to do. He asks the children what they normally do in Sunday school. He wonders what subject to do today. He fumbles in his pocket and pulls out crumpled letters or pictures. He pins these on the board in the wrong order. For example, LISARE. With the children's help rearrange to ISRAEL. Mr Weak and Wobbly struggles off. Leader 2 comes on.

Today's true story from the Bible is about someone who was called by God to do a special job, but was very unsure that he was able to do it. Come back and tell me:

1. What was the man's name?

2. What was he asked to do?

3. How did God show him he was the right man for the job?

CONSOLIDATION 2

A team racing game from one end of the room to the other. Place a strong blanket in the middle to be the fleece. Either time each team, in which case only one blanket is required, or have one blanket per team if all race at the same time. The first race, the children run to the fleece, roll across it, then run to the end. The second race, the children hop to the blanket, crawl under the fleece (with leaders holding up the ends), then hop to the end. The third race, the children crawl to the fleece, bunny hop across it, then crawl to the end.

WIND UP 2

Review the questions from the Warm Up. Remind the children that, although Gideon was unsure of himself, he was certain about God. He trusted God, even though his family did not. God called him to help and lead his people. God used the fleece to help Gideon to trust him for his special job. Gideon obeyed God.

VICTORY GIVEN

Text: Read and study Judges 7:1-25.

Memory Verse: Not by might, nor by power, but by my Spirit, says the Lord Almighty. Zech 4:6

Teaching point: Success in God's work only comes from doing things God's way.

WARM UP 1

The object is to demonstrate that you can only achieve your aim if you do it the right way. One small child tries to pull the leader on a sack (or bath towel or in a washing basket or similar container). Then 2-3 children try to pull the leader on the sack. Then one leader tries to pull the leader on the sack. (Make sure the leader is big enough for all to fail.) Finally two leaders try and pull the leader on the sack and they achieve their object. Point out to the children that different tasks need different abilities. You had to be strong enough to pull the leader on the sack.

Today's true story from the Bible is about a task that God set Gideon. Come back and tell me:

1. What was the task?

2. What did Gideon **not** need to complete that task?

3. How did God show Gideon what he **did** need?

CONSOLIDATION 1

The object of the game is to collect the words to make up the memory verse by asking questions based on today's Bible story. The memory verse is, *'Not by might, nor by power, but by my Spirit,' says the Lord Almighty. Zechariah 4:6.* Divide the verse and reference into 9 sections and write one section on each strip of paper. You require one set for each team. Place each strip of paper in an envelope and mark the envelope with a symbol, such as square, circle, triangle. Designate 9 different areas and place one envelope of each symbol in each area. Prepare 9 questions and answers about the Bible story. After each question designate which area the child must visit to pick up his team's envelope.

Rules:

1. Each child in the team must answer at least 1 question and collect an answer. Younger children can have an adult with them. Make sure the younger children answer the easy questions!

2. Questions are asked one at a time. When a child gives a correct answer, he or she is told to go to a destination and pick up an envelope with the team symbol on it. The next question can only be asked once the child has returned with the envelope.

3. The winning team is the one that collects all the words of the memory verse and puts them in the correct order. If there is only a small number of children, keep them as one group. If playing in teams, class teachers could swap groups for the quiz.

WIND UP 1

The game involved listening to instructions and doing what was said. Review the questions from the Warm Up. Gideon had to listen to God and do what he said. Success in God's work only comes from doing things God's way. God requires his people to be obedient.

VICTORY GIVEN

Text: Read and study Judges 7:1-25.

Memory Verse: Not by might, nor by power, but by my Spirit, says the Lord Almighty. Zech 4:6

Teaching point: Success in God's work only comes from doing things God's way.

WARM UP 2

Announce you are a great athlete. Challenge the children to touch the ceiling by stretching. Announce you are also a great magician. Challenge the children to make a friend disappear. Announce you are a great mathematician. Challenge the children to do a difficult sum immediately. Write on the board 148828 ÷ 5132. (The answer is 29.)

Recap on the challenges. Show them that you can do them (by cheating). To touch the ceiling, stand on a chair and use a pole. To make a friend disappear, say Leader 2 is a friend and then send him into another room. To complete the sum, produce the answer already written on paper. Ask

the children if they are impressed with your abilities. You cannot do the impossible and neither can the children.

In today's true story from the Bible we will see how God enabled his people to do something which was humanly impossible. Come back and tell me:

1. What was the impossible task? *(To beat the Midianites with so few soldiers.)*

2. How did God bring it about?

CONSOLIDATION 2

Play this game in class groups. Devise a series of questions and answers on the lesson, age specific for the classes. You need at least 8 questions for each group. The right answer gains the team a letter. The letters are G I D E O N in that order. Each letter equals a stepping-stone to get the team to the Midianite camp and victory. The teams also have the option of choosing a mystery envelope instead of their next letter. The envelope may contain, 'lose 1 letter', 'lose 2 letters', 'God's way - gain 1 letter', 'God's way - gain two letters'. Lost letters are replaced with the remaining letters to be won. The first team to make GIDEON crosses all its members to the Midianite camp and wins the battle.

WIND UP 2

Review the questions from the Warm Up. Remind the children of the odds - Midianites 22,000:Israelites 300 - and the Israelites did not even have to fight! It was impossible for men by themselves, but no problem to God, because God can do anything. Remind the children of the memory verse: *'Not by might, nor by power, but by my Spirit,' says the Lord Almighty. Zechariah 4:6.* All the people had to do was to obey God's word.

THE STRONG MAN

Text: Read and study Judges 13:1-10,24-25; 14:1 - 15:15.

Teaching Point: To reinforce the story details.

WARM UP 1

Prior to the children's arrival place the following objects on a table: a jar of honey, a toy lion, a piece of cloth (ideally doll's clothing) to represent a wedding garment, a lock of hair, a bone. Cover each object with a pot or small bucket.

By a series of qualifications, eliminate all but one child, e.g. all who are born in July stay in, all who have black hair, all who are wearing trainers, etc. Start with the children standing. As people are eliminated they sit down. The winner chooses one pot and reveals the first object. Repeat for the other objects.

All these objects are featured in today's true story from the Bible. Come back and tell me where they fit in.

CONSOLIDATION 1

Which class will be the weakest link? Devise a series of questions on the Bible story (you need as many as possible). The children play in class groups. The aim is to see which class's Samson kills the most Philistines. Pin up a scoreboard (see diagram). Each class needs a paper Samson (see picture on page 37) that can be moved along the board. Samson moves up one number with each correct answer.

The winner is the class whose Samson has killed the most Philistines.

WIND UP 1

Review the objects in the Warm Up. How did each one fit into the story? Link in to the game. Why was Samson so strong? Because God was with him.

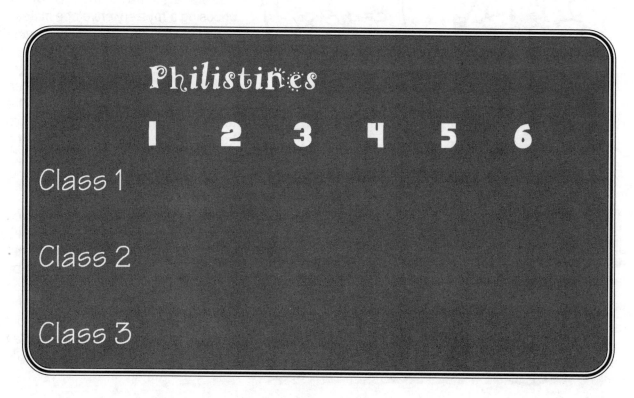

THE STRONG MAN

Text: Read and study Judges 13:1-10,24-25; 14:1 - 15:15.

Teaching Point: To show how God chose a deliverer for his people.

WARM UP 2

The leader announces that he is a famous strong man, Mr Zappo. Mr Zappo challenges the children to do the following:

1. Move a wall by leaning on it.

2. Pick up a car with one hand.

3. Push the floor down.

The children attempt the tasks one by one and fail. Zappo produces a picture of a wall, a toy car and a picture of the floor. He completes the tasks.

Today's true story from the Bible is about a man who was really very strong, not like Mr Zappo. Come back and tell me:

1. What was his name?

2. What things could he **not** do?

3. What was the secret of his great strength?

CONSOLIDATION 2

Choose a number of tasks for the children to perform, such as arrange plastic toy animals neatly, build a house from Lego or building bricks, build a tower from plastic cups, etc. Before they finish each task move them on to the next thing.

Round up by explaining that you are going to lay the table for supper. Carry the tray of cutlery half way to the table, look round and talk about the need for glasses, drop the cutlery and get plastic glasses. Realise you have forgotten the plates, drop the glasses and get the plates. Does the table look good?

Point out that they were unable to complete their tasks because they were distracted by being moved on to other tasks. You could not lay the table properly because you were distracted by thinking of other things. In the same way, Samson was distracted by many things from doing what God wanted.

WIND UP 2

Review the questions from the Warm Up. God was with Samson because he wanted to rescue his people, but did he approve of all the things Samson did?

THE ENEMY DEFEATED

Text: Read and study Judges 16:1-31.

Teaching Point: Sin has consequences.

WARM UP 1

Tell the children that you have prepared a surprise for them. Because they are so good and helpful you have decided to reward them with a special treat. You went out and bought some really delicious chocolate biscuits for them to have at the end of their Bible story. So that they can look forward to the treat you will show them the biscuits. You left them on a tray just over there (point to a tray covered with a cloth). Ask one of the leaders to get the tray. Take the cloth off the tray and reveal nothing apart from a few crumbs. Where are the biscuits? Who has taken them? Ask various children and leaders if they have taken the biscuits, or if they know who has taken them. Say that you cannot proceed until the culprit owns up. One of the leaders starts to shuffle around, then develops stomachache. Ask that leader if he took the biscuits. Eventually he owns up to eating all of them. They looked and tasted so good that he just could not resist them. Then he says he is going to be sick and rushes out of the room. Point out that he gave in to temptation and the consequences are that he is feeling very unwell, as well as being in disgrace.

In today's true story from the Bible we will find out what happened to Samson when he gave in to temptation. Come back and tell me:

1. What wrong things did Samson do?

2. What were the consequences?

CONSOLIDATION 1

The object is to demonstrate the importance of running away from sin or danger.

Prepare pictures of a snake, 7 bowstrings, ropes, and hair (see page 39). Show them to the children and tell them that they are all symbols of temptation. Place them with blank sheets of paper in a bucket to one side. Place a parachute or sheet in the middle of the area. The children form a circle around the parachute. The children move around the circle in the same direction while the music plays. When the music stops the child closest to the bucket picks out a sheet of paper. If it is blank the music starts and the children move in a circle around the parachute. If the sheet of paper has a picture on it the children run into the centre and hide under the parachute. The last one under the parachute is sent to the 'Sin Bin' and misses one turn. Occasionally change the direction in which the children move around the circle.

WIND UP 1

Remind the children of the Warm Up. Sin has consequences. Review the questions from the Warm Up. Talk about the game. What did they do when temptation occurred? They ran away from it. What happened to the last person? They went to the 'Sin Bin'. Remind them that Samson gave in to temptation and the consequences were terrible. But that was not the end of the story. When he turned back to God for help, God helped him. When we do naughty things, if we are truly sorry and ask God to forgive us he will do so.

THE ENEMY DEFEATED

Text: Read and study Judges 16:1-31.

Teaching Point: Sin has consequences.

WARM UP 2

This is designed to remind the children of Samson's Nazirite vow and how he broke it the previous lesson. It can be done as a skit or as puppets (see script on page 79-80). You also need pictures of a wine goblet, grapes, long hair and a dead body (see pages 38-39).

Toby and Trudy are visiting Sunday School. Toby says he was there the previous week and it was so good that he has brought Trudy with him this week. Toby says he told Trudy what happened in last week's story. The leader asks Trudy questions about the story as a review. Trudy remembers as far as Samson being unable to drink alcohol. Toby asks the leader to pin up the pictures to help Trudy remember. They finish by going through the parts of the Nazirite vow that Samson did not keep. Each time the leader puts a cross through the appropriate picture. The only picture without a cross is the picture of long hair. The leader sends the children off to Bible time with the following questions:

1. Is Samson going to break any part of the promise this week?

2. If so, which bits?

The puppets remain visible until the children have gone.

CONSOLIDATION 2

The aim of the game is to demonstrate that behaviour has consequences. You need one mat for each child plus eight extra, eight pictures - two each of bowstrings, new ropes, long hair woven into a loom, seven locks of hair (see pictures on page 39). Fix the eight pictures to the underside of eight of the mats. Place the mats around the room with the eight picture mats scattered randomly among the other mats. Show the children which mats have pictures underneath. The children move around the room to music. When the music stops each child must stand on a mat, avoiding the picture mats. Any child standing on a picture mat is out.

WIND UP 2

Talk about the Warm Up and go over the two questions the children were sent to class with. Talk about the game. Any child standing on a picture mat was out - they did not avoid what they knew to be wrong. Talk about the four pictures and Samson playing with temptation. By allowing Delilah to cut off his hair Samson was severing his covenant with God, and the result was that God left him (Judges 16:20). Samson's disobedience had consequences. Likewise, when Samson repented and turned back to God, God heard and answered his prayer (Judges 16:28).

RUTH AND NAOMI

Text: Read and study Ruth 1:1-22.

Teaching point: How Ruth came to trust God.

WARM UP 1

What do you need to go on a journey? Have some things ready: food, drink, tent, matches, Primus stove, sleeping bag, etc. Write up others on a board. What would Old Testament people have had?

In today's true story from the Bible we will find out about some people who made a journey to another country, then later on returned to their own country. I want you to come back and tell me:

1. Who made the original journey?

2. Why did they leave their own country?

3. Who came back?

CONSOLIDATION 1

Divide the children into two teams with an equal split of ages. The older children form pairs and kneel down facing each other. They lean forwards with their hands on each other's shoulders to form an arch. Line them up to form a tunnel. The younger ones race to crawl underneath. The first team to get all the younger children through the tunnel wins.

At the end reinforce the following: the older children had to trust each other to keep upright and the younger children had to trust the older children not to collapse on them. I can trust God to look after me, just as he looked after Ruth.

WIND UP 1

Review the questions from the Warm Up. Remind the children of the journey preparations in the Warm Up. Did Ruth and Naomi have all these? Possibly, but not much food or future. How would they live when they got there? Remind the children of the game and how they had to trust each other. Ruth and Naomi had to learn to trust God.

RUTH AND NAOMI

Text: Read and study Ruth 1:1-22.

Teaching point: How Ruth came to trust God.

WARM UP 2

The leader enters wearing dark glasses and carrying a white cane. He announces that he is called Ian Charles Badleigh, normally called I C Badleigh. He had a terrible time getting here. He got on the wrong bus, walked up the wrong road and ended up at a local shop. He even went in and asked where the hymnbook (or service sheet) was. He says that he has a very important collection of bits from repairing his car safely on a tray somewhere. The tray has been previously arranged just balancing on the edge of the table. The leader increases the tension with near misses, eventually knocking the tray and contents over the floor. The leader ends by saying that it's important to see where we're going.

Today's true story from the Bible is about some ladies who took a journey. Come back and tell me:

1. What were the two ladies' names?

2. Where were they coming from?

3. Where were they going to?

CONSOLIDATION 2

A reverse relay. Set out side boundaries with rope or string and optional lane markers 0.75 metres wide. Divide the children into teams. Children start from both ends, with half the team at each end. Have a relay race, performing all events backwards. Events can include running, hopping, bottom shuffling, etc. Make sure you are safe.

WIND UP 2

Remind the children of the importance of seeing where you are going, e.g. on the way to school, in the playground, collecting school meals, etc. Review the questions from the Warm Up. It was difficult for Ruth because she did not know where she was going, what was going to happen and how she would live when she arrived. But she trusted God for the future, even though she could not see it.

RUTH AND BOAZ

Text: Read and study Ruth 2:1 - 4:22.

Teaching point: God takes care of those who trust him.

WARM UP 1

Set out six matchboxes on a table. Prior to the lesson mark one so that you can easily identify it. Place a small harmless insect in it (or a plastic one). Ask the children to guess what the matchboxes contain. Accept suggestions. Tell them that one box has your pet in it.

Produce samples of hay, straw, unlikely food such as doughnut, tinned food, jam, etc. and its unlikely drink such as vinegar. Can the children guess what your pet is?

Tell them that you will show them the pet if they can guess which box it is in. The children guess which box contains the pet. Mix the boxes around to confuse the issue. After each guess, show them an empty box. Eventually disclose the insect.

Say that today's true story from the Bible is about God looking after someone much more important than even the best pet.

I want you to come back and tell me:

1. Who did God look after?

2. How did he look after her?

CONSOLIDATION 1

Divide the children into 'family groups of one or two older children and some younger ones. Place the older children under a table at the far end of the room. In the centre of the room, place a large box of finely shredded paper or mixed breakfast cereals, rice, etc. Provide the older children with a disposable drinking cup or similar size container. Provide the other children with a small lid or bottle cap to collect the cereal mix in. The object of the game is for the younger children to collect the cereal mix in their small measuring scoop or lid, take it to the older children under the table and empty it into the older children's disposable cups until they are full. The older children are not to move from their set location.

The younger children will have to make repeated visits to the cereal mix box and should be reminded to care for one another as they fill up their small lids. The first team to fill the older children's disposable cups wins. If time permits, choose another group of children to be stranded and to be cared for by the other children.

WIND UP 1

Remind the children about your pet in the matchbox. Go over the game and how the younger children cared for the older ones. Review the questions from the Warm Up.

RUTH AND BOAZ

Text: Read and study Ruth 2:1 - 4:22.

Memory Verse: Trust in God, and he will help you. Psalm 37:5

Teaching point: God takes care of those who trust him.

WARM UP 2

The leader has several objects in his pockets and some on the table. While talking about the importance of caring for one another, a leader in the role of 'Mr Creepy' creeps round behind the leader. Mr Creepy starts picking the leader's pockets and taking things from the table. The leader is oblivious to what is happening. Eventually the leader notices what is going on. Mr Creepy confesses, but says he was just 'looking after' the things to keep them safe. The leader is not sure about this; he will have a think about it and let the children know later.

Today's true story from the Bible is about someone who really did look after someone else. Come back and tell me:

1. Who was looked after?

2. Who did the looking after?

3. How did he look after the other person?

CONSOLIDATION 2

Hide and seek. Children hunt for words on card to form, 'Trust in God, and he will help you. Psalm 37:5.' Hide the words around the room. Divide the children into teams and give each group a base. All but two members of each team hunt for the words. The two stay at the base to make up the sentence. Once most teams have collected three or four words, the leader, says 'Raid!' One of the team members at the base can raid other bases for missing words. Only one team member can raid and he can only collect one word per raid. The sentence maker at base cannot prevent other raiders from raiding his base. Assign one leader per base to ensure fair play. Other team members can only hunt for words, not raid. The sentence maker and raider can swap places. The winner is the first team to complete their verse.

WIND UP 2

Recap on the Warm Up. Was Mr Creepy a good example of caring for one another? No. He was not really looking after things. Review the questions from the Warm Up. God looked after Ruth by providing food, shelter, protection and a husband. God will also look after us when we trust him. Repeat the memory verse.

SAMUEL, A PRECIOUS BABY

Text: Read and study 1 Samuel 1:1-28; 2:11,18-21.

Memory verse: Trust in God, and he will help you. Psalm 37:5.

Teaching Point: God answers the prayers of those who trust him.

WARM UP 1

Show the children some baby clothes and equipment. Talk about babies and let the children suggest what each item is used for. For example, sun hat (no hair), bottle (cannot use a cup, cannot eat at first). Talk about how parents spend lots of time looking after their baby, mums do not like leaving their babies. Draw attention to how much they love the baby and how precious the baby is to them.

In today's true story from the Bible there is a lady who is very sad because she hasn't got a baby. Come back and tell me:

1. What was the lady's name?

2. What did she promise God?

3. What was the baby's name?

CONSOLIDATION 1

The object is to reinforce that Hannah had to wait patiently for God to act. Divide the children into groups. Select one person to be the game piece. Give each group a large rubber dice (pet toys). The groups take it in turns to throw the dice. The number thrown allows the game piece to take that number of steps. The game pieces advance until all reach the end of the course. There are no winners! Some have to wait a little longer than the others.

WIND UP 1

Remind the children of the Warm Up. Review the questions. Refer to the game. Hannah had to wait patiently for God to act. She was not sad any more because she knew God would answer her prayer.

WARM UP 2

Ask your church and Sunday School leaders to supply you with pictures of them as babies. Display them on a board and ask the children to guess who they are. Talk about how everyone was a baby once - wore nappies, rode in a pram, was rocked to sleep by mother.

In today's true story from the Bible there is a baby who had a very unusual childhood. Come back and tell me:

1. What was the name of the baby?

2. What was the name of his mum?

3. What was unusual about his childhood?

CONSOLIDATION 2

The children work in teams. Each team has a 'washing line' made of string and pegs. The memory verse is written on coloured paper. Each word is written on a different coloured robe shape. The shapes get smaller towards the end of the verse (see diagram page 37). You need one set for each team. Hide the robes around the room. Each team has to find one robe of each colour, arrange them in order of size and peg them on the washing line. If they do this in the correct order they will find their memory verse. The first team to manage this is the winner.

WIND UP 2

Review the questions from the Warm Up. God answered Hannah's prayer and she kept her promise. Remind the children that Hannah took a new robe for Samuel each year when she visited him at the temple. What did the children find when they collected all the robes? Repeat the memory verse.

SAMUEL, AN OBEDIENT BOY

Text: Read and study 1 Samuel 3:1-21.

Teaching Point: The need to listen to God's word and do what he says.

WARM UP 1

Display a number of objects that pertain to listening and hearing. These can include the following:

plastic ears, stethoscope, tape cassette, microphone, headphones, hearing aid, radio.

Talk about the different objects and show the children how they work. Point out that it is possible to do things to prevent your hearing something. Then try actions that shut out sounds, such as put on earmuffs, hat over ears, ear plugs, hands over ears. Play music while this is going on.

Today's true story is about a little boy who did not recognise what he heard. Come back and tell me:

1. What was the boy's name?

2. Who spoke to him?

3. Who did he think was speaking?

CONSOLIDATION 1

All the children lie on the floor with their eyes closed. The leader has a bag containing pieces of paper with each child's name on them. The leader pulls out a piece of paper and calls the child's name softly. The child responds by getting up quietly and sitting down beside the leader. If the child does not respond, move on to the next name. If a child responds wrongly send them back to lie down.

This could also be played as a team game. The first team to collect all its members calls out, 'Samuel!'

WIND UP 1

Remind the children of the Warm Up and how we can block out sound. Review the questions. Refer to the game and the importance of listening carefully. Then ask, 'How do we listen to God's voice?' Through reading his word, the Bible, and having it explained to us.

SAMUEL, AN OBEDIENT BOY

Text: Read and study 1 Samuel 3:1-21.

Teaching Point: The need to listen to God's word and do what he says.

WARM UP 2

Ask for a volunteer to be blindfolded. Tell the group that when you point to individuals they are to call out '*(Name, Name)*, who am I?' After each person has called out ask, 'Can you recognise who is calling out to you?' Allow 6 calls. Persons to call out can include the main leader, siblings, friends, own class leader, other leader, unknown parent, unknown child, etc. Remove the blindfold and tell the volunteer how many he got right. Repeat with one or two other volunteers. Then lead in to a brief discussion by asking, 'Who does he recognise?' 'Why does he recognise the voice?' *(He knows them already.)*

Today's true story from the Bible is about someone who was called by name and did not recognise the caller. Come back and tell me:

1. Who was being called?

2. Who was doing the calling?

3. How many times was he called?

4. Why wasn't the caller recognised?

CONSOLIDATION 2

Designate four areas numbered 1 to 4. The children lie down on the floor in the middle of the room and listen to the number of times the whistle is blown. If the whistle is blown once, the children run to the area designated 1; if the whistle is blown twice, the children run to the area designated 2, etc. In between the whistle blowing the children return to the centre and lie down. Those running to different areas are out of the game or sent to the 'Sin Bin' to miss a set number of turns.

WIND UP 2

Review the questions from the Warm Up. Remind the children of the Warm Up and how difficult it was for the volunteer to recognise the voice of someone he did not know. In the same way it was difficult for Samuel to recognise God's voice. He needed Eli to help him. Is it important that we recognise God's voice? Refer to the game and what happened to those who got it wrong. How do we listen to God's voice? Through reading his word, the Bible, and having it explained to us.

SAUL SEARCHES FOR DONKEYS

Text: Read and study 1 Samuel 8:1 - 9:26.

Teaching Point: The importance of making right choices.

WARM UP 1

Offer the children the choice of watching a video or having a Bible story. Show them a collection of videocassettes of suitable children's titles in attractively packaged boxes. Ask what they want to do. When they choose watching a video, open the chosen video box and set up the cassette on a table at the front. Sit down and pretend to read a book. When disappointment or boredom sets in ask if they made a good choice. Was it as good as they expected?

In today's true story from the Bible people made a bad choice. Come back and tell me:

1. Who were the people?

2. What choice did they make?

3. Why was it a bad choice? *(They rejected God as their king.)*

CONSOLIDATION 1

Divide the children into teams. The same number of different items as teams are placed on a chair or table some distance from the children. The items could be anything such as balls, plastic toys, cups, etc. The leader decides privately which is the winning item.

Each team selects a runner. The runner runs down to the chair or table, picks up an item and goes back to their team. The leader says which was the winning item. The team who have it keep it and the remaining items are returned to the chair or table and another item is added. The leader decides which one is the winning item and different children run up and make their selection. The winning team has the most items in their possession at the end. The leader needs to keep emphasising 'choice' and who made the right one.

WIND UP 1

Remind the children of the Warm Up and how easy it is to make bad choices. Refer to the game and point out how difficult it was to make the right choice when they did not know what the leader was thinking. Review the questions from the Warm Up. Did the Israelites make the wrong choice because they did not know what God wanted?

SAUL SEARCHES FOR DONKEYS

Text: Read and study 1 Samuel 8:1 - 9:26.

Teaching Point: The stupidity of insisting on your own way rather than God's.

WARM UP 2

Someone dressed as a doctor enters the room. A sick boy is there with a nurse. The doctor asks for the case history, which is told by the nurse. The boy asked his mum for chocolates. She refused and said it was no good for him. He persisted, but she still refused. He threw a tantrum. Still she said no, it would not be good for him. He started to rave and threaten. She finally gave in. He ate 12 cream eggs and got very sick. She warned him of the consequences of what would happen. He did not take any notice. Now look at him. Pain, discomfort, distress, cream egg poisoning. In today's true story from the Bible there is something similar happening. Come back and tell me:

1. Who wanted something they should not have?

2. Who gave it to them?

3. Why was it going to be bad for them?

CONSOLIDATION 2

Divide the children into two groups and assign a leader to each. Give each leader strips of paper with an action written on each. The first team leader picks an action for the team to do while the other team watches. If the onlookers think that the action is good, they copy it. If they think it is bad, they turn their backs on the team doing the action. Then the second team has a go. Repeat turn and turn about until all the actions have been performed. Suitable actions to include are: clap and cheer, dance, crawl from one end of the room to the other, do star jumps, lie on the floor and throw a tantrum, point at the other team and jeer, tear up a newspaper, etc. Make sure that both teams have a mix of good and bad actions.

WIND UP 2

Remind the children of the Warm Up and how silly it was for the boy to persist in having his own way. Review the questions from the Warm Up. Why did the people want to have a king? Because they wanted to be like everyone else. Refer to the game and how they decided whether or not to copy the other team.

CREAM EGG POISONING

SAUL MADE KING

Text: Read and study 1 Samuel 9:26 - 10:27

Teaching Point: God sometimes allows us to have our own way to teach us a lesson.

WARM UP 1

Ask 'What does a shepherd do?' He looks after sheep. He guides them to water and feed. He anticipates danger and steers the sheep away from it. He shelters them at night. He makes sure they stay healthy because they are precious to him. How does a shepherd control the sheep? Sometimes he uses sheep dogs. He tells the dogs what to do by shouting instructions that they understand. Sometimes he uses a whistle. Blow the whistle. One short blast for 'right', two short blasts for 'left', one long blast for 'stop - lie on ground', two long blasts for 'go forward'. Tell the children what the signals mean. Tell the children to get down on all fours and practise responding to the whistle. Ask the children if they have ever seen sheepdogs herding sheep. Do the sheep always do what the dogs want? The sheep often try and go their own way. In today's true story from the Bible we will see how God was still in control of what happened to his people, even when they made bad decisions. Come back and tell me:

1. What was the bad decision the people made from last week? *(They wanted a king like everyone else, rejecting God as their king.)*

2. What happened in the story to show that God was still in control?

CONSOLIDATION 1

The object is to demonstrate the benefit of having someone in control. Use chairs as a sheep pen at one end of the room. Remind the children about the way the shepherd controls his dogs with a whistle. Practise responding to the whistle. Ask for volunteers to be sheep dogs. The rest of the children will be the sheep. Have some fun trying to get the sheep into the pen. If time permits repeat the game using different sheepdogs.

WIND UP 1

Remind the children of the Warm Up and the benefit of having someone in control. Refer to the game. Even though it was chaotic at times, the shepherd knew what was happening and was in control. Review the questions from the Warm Up. Remind the children that God was still in control, even though his people had rejected him as their king. He was the one who provided their king. In later years the Israelites would discover that having a king caused problems, just as God had said it would (1 Samuel 8:10-18).

SAUL MADE KING

Text: Read and study 1 Samuel 9:26 - 10:27

Teaching Point: God sometimes allows us to have our own way to teach us a lesson.

Lesson 10

WARM UP 2

Tell the children you have done some swapping you are really pleased with. Show them a toy car. You have swapped your real car for this. Show them a plastic model of a person. You have swapped your friend for this. Show them a tiny chocolate sweet. You have swapped your biggest box of chocolates for this. Explain that, although these things are small, you are very pleased with them because you'll be the same as everyone else now. Explain that, although they can't do what the things you swapped them for can do, it's worth it to be the same as everyone else.

Ask what big thing the Israelites swapped for a little thing, i.e. their king. Draw attention to what an earthly king could not do compared with God. Ask if it was sensible choice.

In today's true story from the Bible we see how it works out. Come back and tell me:

1. How did Saul know that he was God's choice?

2. How did the people know that Saul was God's choice?

CONSOLIDATION 2

Someone is Saul. He goes off to hide. The rest of the children are divided into teams, each designated by a colour. Give each team a crown in their colour. The teams hunt for 'Saul'. When Saul is found, that team crowns him with their crown and brings him back to their home base. Someone from the winning team is chosen as the next 'Saul' and the game continues.

WIND UP 2

Remind the children of the Warm Up and how silly it was to swap something big for something little just to be the same as everyone else. What did the Israelites swap? But God gave them what they asked for. Review the questions from the Warm Up. Everything looked good. Ask the children why Saul looked like a good king. However, in later years the Israelites would discover that having a king caused problems, just as God had said it would (1 Samuel 8:10-18).

SAUL OFFERS THE SACRIFICE

Text: Read and study 1 Samuel 13:1-16; 14:1-23.

Teaching point: The importance of obeying God.

WARM UP 1

Tell the children they are to have obedience training. One whistle - stand still, two whistles - lie down, three whistles - stand on one leg. Repeat at random. It's important to know how to obey. In today's true story from the Bible we see what happened when someone disobeyed God. Come back and tell me:

1. Who was it who disobeyed?

2. How did he disobey?

3. What was the result?

CONSOLIDATION 1

The aim is to demonstrate the importance of following instructions and the consequences of disobedience. Place a sheet or parachute in the centre of the room to be the home base. Mark out an area to the side to be the 'Sin Bin'. Designate 4 points around the sides of the room to be North, South, East and West. The children start at base. Decide beforehand whether the children sit on top of the sheet or get underneath it. The leader shouts out a compass point and the children run to it. Anyone going to the wrong point is sent to the 'Sin Bin' for a set number of turns. Once the children have got the game sorted, change it by sending different class groups to different locations at the same time.

WIND UP 1

Talk about the importance of obedience and the consequences of disobedience, referring to both the Warm Up and the Consolidation. Review the questions from the Warm Up.

WARM UP 2

Choose a small child and pretend you are afraid of them. Explain why they are very scary, such as huge muscles, superhuman strength, fierce smile, etc. and keep asking the little one, 'You won't hurt me, will you?' Meanwhile Leader 2 is creeping around trying to harm Leader 1 by hitting him with a blow up hammer or baseball bat or similar. Leader 1 takes no notice of Leader 2 until leader 2 bops him on the head. Point out that you were afraid of the wrong person. In today's true story from the Bible King Saul shows that he's afraid of the wrong person. Come back and tell me:

1. Who is he afraid of?

2. Who should he be afraid of?

CONSOLIDATION 2

Put a pile of equipment in the middle of the room, such as safe cooking equipment, teacher's equipment, postman's equipment (bag, letters), window cleaner's (cloth and bucket), etc. Photocopy cards with cook, teacher, postman, window cleaner. If the children cannot read use pictures. You need enough cards for each child to have one. Deal out the cards. The children move around the pile of equipment to music. When the music stops they have to find something for the character on their card, e.g. a saucepan for the cook. When they get the hang of this collect the cards and reallocate. People can be out for having inappropriate equipment for their character.

WIND UP 2

Refer to the game. Each person had a job and they were only allowed to get the equipment for that person. Give examples of equipment which wasn't allowed. In today's story someone did a job he wasn't allowed to do. Who was that? Who was allowed to do that job? *(The Priest.)* Why did Saul do it? Review the questions from the Warm Up.

SAUL DISOBEYS GOD

Text: Read and study 1 Samuel 15:1-35.

Teaching Point: The result of repeated disobedience

WARM UP 1

The Warm Up is dealing with two elements: repeated disobedience and clothing being torn to signify the kingdom being taken from Saul.

Tell the children about something that has happened to you during the week. While this is going on leader two takes shirts out of a bag, puts them on coat hangers and hangs them up on a rail or line. Leader 2 makes as much noise as possible each time a shirt is pulled out of a bag or hung up. It would be helpful to have some bright shirts, as these would be even more distracting. Ask Leader 2 to stop because it is very distracting and no one can hear the story. Leader 2 stops for a few seconds only, then returns to the activity, making even more noise than before. This is repeated three or four times until the last shirt has been hung up. Leader 1 becomes more and more irritated. While the last shirt is being shaken out, a part of the shirt that is badly torn comes off. Leader 2 is very upset.

In today's true story from the Bible we will see disobedience and a torn garment. Come back and tell me:

1. Who disobeyed?
2. How did he disobey?
3. What did the torn garment signify?

CONSOLIDATION 1

Give two leaders or older children a sheet or pillowcase to hold at each end. They have to chase the other children and surround them with the sheet by joining hands. The caught children go into a pen. The people holding the sheet are referred to as the 'Israelites' and the rest are 'Amalekites'. When all are caught ask:

1. What did God tell Saul to do with the Amalekites?
2. What did Saul do?

Then release some, giving them appropriate names. Repeat with different 'Israelites', going through the same procedure when all are penned. If you have a large number of children you may need more than one pair of Israelites.

WIND UP 1

What instructions did God give to Saul? Did they capture all the Amalekites like we did in the game? Review the questions from the Warm Up.

SAUL DISOBEYS GOD

Text: Read and study 1 Samuel 15:1-35.

Teaching Point: The result of repeated disobedience

WARM UP 2

Give the children several commands. Some nice, such as have a sweet; some neutral, such as stand on one leg, lie on the floor; some not nice, such as give me back the sweets, clean up every speck of dirt on the floor. Ask in turn which were easy and which hard to obey. (The instructions could be written on cards and placed in two piles or stuck up in two different places.)

Draw attention to the fact that obedience is only difficult if you do not want to do what is asked, or if you do not agree with what is asked. (A good example for adults is the speed limit.) Then it is difficult to obey.

Today's true story from the Bible is about a man who only wanted to obey God when he agreed with what God said. Come back and tell me what happened when God told him to do something he didn't want to do.

CONSOLIDATION 2

Balloon football. Divide the children into two teams. The teams line up opposite each other, then sit down with their feet facing at least three metres apart. One team is the Israelites, the other one is the Amalekites. The leader tosses a balloon into the centre of the teams. Each team tries to score goals by batting the balloon over the heads of the opposing team. The children have to remain sitting. Towards the end of the game the leader joins the Israelites' side to make them win.

WIND UP 2

The Israelites won because God was on their side (like the leader helping the Israelites in the Consolidation). What did God tell them to do to the Amalekites? Did they do what God said? Why not?

GOD SEES EVERYTHING

Text: Read and study 1 Samuel 16:1-23.

Memory verse: 'Man looks at the outward appearance, but God looks at the heart.' 1Samuel 16:7

Teaching Point: God sees the heart and nothing can be hidden from him.

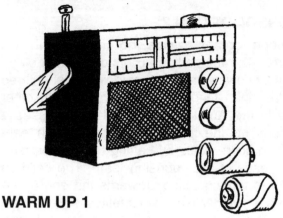

WARM UP 1

Display some containers, i.e. video game, radio, box of sweets, book, moneybag. The contents are not what are suggested by the outsides. The video game is empty, the radio has no batteries, the sweet box contains scraps of paper, the moneybag contains plastic money. The inside of the book has been hollowed out to make a secret compartment. Inside it is the memory verse: *1 Samuel 16:7.* (An interesting empty food container could be used instead of a book.) Ask for volunteers. Ask them to go and stand by the item of their choice. Ask the children to open them one by one to see that the inside does not match the outside. Isn't it easy to be fooled by appearances? Open the book and read out the verse. If the book has been chosen, open that last. Today's true Bible story is about choosing a new king. Come back and tell me:

1. Who was chosen?
2. How was he chosen?

CONSOLIDATION 1

The aim is to demonstrate the importance of choices. Divide the children into teams. Appoint a location for each team's base. Tell them that one of them is 'David'. Only the leader know who David is. They must discover David and bring him onto their team. Allocate a leader to each team. Each team takes it in turn to decide how many people between one and three they want to exchange. On the command, 'Change!' each leader takes that number of children into the centre, calling out the number and exchanges them for that number from another team. The leader states which team David is in. Repeat the exchange procedure. State which team David is in now. Repeat until David has been identified. In order to win the team has to identify David and have him in their team.

WIND UP 1

Remind the children of the Warm Up and how easy it is to be fooled by appearances. Was it easy to identify David in the Consolidation? Review the questions from the Warm Up.

WARM UP 2

Show the children some exotic fruit. Ask each time, 'What does it look like inside? Is it sweet or sour to taste?' Cut open the fruit and show the children what it looks like. Give them some to taste. Point out that we can't tell what the inside is like from looking on the outside. Today's true story from the Bible is about how God chose a new king. Come back and tell me:

1. Who was chosen?
2. Why was he chosen?

CONSOLIDATION 2

Divide the children into teams. Prepare a set of different coloured hearts for each team with a word of the memory verse on each heart. Place each heart in a container and place all the containers in the centre of the room. The team members take it in turns to run into the centre, pick up a container and return to base. If the container has the team colour heart in it, retain it. If not, return it to the centre with the next child to run. The winner is the first team to collect their hearts and place the memory verse in the correct order.

WIND UP 2

Remind the children about the Warm Up and how impossible it is to know what is on the inside from looking at the outside. Review the questions. Link in to the game. Repeat the memory verse.

GOD RESCUES HIS PEOPLE

Text: Read and study 1 Samuel 17:1-53.

Memory verse: *Man looks at the outward appearance, but God looks at the heart. 1 Samuel 16:7.*

Teaching Point: God is a rescuing God.

WARM UP 1

Leader 1 tells the children all about his special friend. He goes through various things the friend is good at. Leader 2 says that the friend is rubbish. He can't do any of those things. Leader 2 can do all of them better. In today's true story from the Bible we will find out what happened when David met someone who thought that God was rubbish. Come back and tell me:

1. What was the name of that person?
2. What happened to him?
3. Why did it happen to him?

CONSOLIDATION 1

Build a hill (a table with a sheet over it) and stand a leader on it so that he is about 3 metres from the ground. Mark out an area for a stream about 2 metres away and place some table tennis balls or balls of newspaper in it to act as stones to be thrown at Goliath on the hill. Give Goliath a helmet and goggles for protection. The children take it in turns to go to the stream, pick up 5 stones and throw them one at a time at Goliath. The remaining children act as Israelites, cheering on the stone thrower. The leader gives a commentary while this is going on. At the end if no child has been able to hit Goliath on the head, a leader does so. Goliath jumps off the table and lies down dead. Remind the children that Goliath defied God and made fun of him, and paid for it.

WIND UP 1

Remind the children of the Warm Up and review the questions. Link in to the Consolidation. Goliath defied God and paid for his mistake. God rescued his people.

WARM UP 2

Which items are connected with the story? Pull out of a treasure chest (or large box) sundry items, some large, some small. Also include a sword and 5 stones. Bring out the items one at a time, asking the children to state whether they think that item is connected with today's true story from the Bible. Place the 'yes' items on one table and the 'no' items on another. At the end give the children the opportunity to change their minds. Tell them that they can come back at the end of the story to see if they were right. After the story go over the items to see which ones were right and how they were connected with the story.

CONSOLIDATION 2

Divide the children into teams and prepare a series of questions from the Bible story, the same number as words in the memory verse. Use the hearts prepared for the previous lesson, Consolidation 2. Start the teams at one end of the room and place one leader for each team with the jumbled up hearts at the other end. Use carpet squares or similar to make stepping-stones for each team from one end of the room to the other. The team members take it in turns to run along the stepping-stones, pick up a heart and return along the stepping-stones to base. The first team to collect their hearts and arrange them in correct verse order wins.

WIND UP 2

Recap on the main story details, using the appropriate items from the treasure chest. Revise the memory verse.

29

DAVID FILLED WITH GOD'S SPIRIT

Text: Read and study 1 Samuel 18:1 - 19:12.

Teaching Point: God was with David but had left Saul.

WARM UP 1

Display a number of containers that are filled with something. Ask the children to tell you what they think is inside each container. Show them if they are right. Sum up by saying that all of these containers are full of something. Today's true story from the Bible is about a person who was filled with something. Come back and tell me what it was. Suggested containers: balloon (filled with air), talcum powder, cereal box, bottle of water, plastic bottle with marbles, bucket with table tennis balls, etc.

CONSOLIDATION 1

A filling game. Divide the children into teams. Each team sits in a long line, one behind the other. At one end is a bucket full of easily transportable items, such as table tennis balls. At the other end is an empty bucket. The contents of the buckets have to be passed one at a time down the line from the full bucket to the empty one. The winner is the first team to transport their items successfully from one bucket to the other.

WIND UP 1

Remind the children about the Warm Up and the different full containers. Review the question. Refer to the game. God took his Spirit away from Saul and gave it to David. Moving the contents of one bucket down the line to the other bucket was a reminder of that.

WARM UP 2

Two leaders have a competition to see who is the greatest. Use various feats of skill. Leader 1 is always better than Leader 2. Leader 2 gets more and more cross and shows how jealous he is of Leader 1. Eventually leader 2 shouts, 'I hate you!' and walks out. In today's true story from the Bible we will see what happened when someone was jealous. Come back and tell me:

1. Who was jealous?

2. Who was he jealous of?

3. What did he do about it?

CONSOLIDATION 2

Run the gauntlet. Divide the children into two teams. One team is Saul and the other is Jonathan. Saul makes two lines facing each other about two metres apart. Spread out until the lines stretch the length of the room. Give the children in the lines table tennis balls or sponge balls to be their spears. Jonathan starts at one end. The children have to run through the middle of the two lines to the other end. The children in Saul throw their missiles and try and hit the children running through the middle. No missile must be thrown above chest height. Any child who is hit is out. Allow the team up to four runs, before changing sides.

WIND UP 2

Remind the children of the Warm Up and review the questions. Link in to the game. Where younger children are involved do remember to point out that the 'jealous' leader was only acting.

DAVID, A LOVING FRIEND

Text: Read and study 1 Samuel 20:1-42.

Teaching Point: What it means to be a friend.

WARM UP 1

Prepare a list of pairs of friends that children will know, such as Mickey and Minnie, Laurel and Hardy, Charlie Brown and Lucy, Snoopy and Woodstock, Adam and Eve, etc. Write each name on a card. Pin up the cards in two lines, with one of each pair in each line. Ask the children to put them into pairs.

Today's true story from the Bible is about a pair of friends. Come back and tell me:

1. What were their names?

2. How did one show his friendship for the other?

3. What did they promise each other?

CONSOLIDATION 1

A gathering game. Place cards containing pictures or symbols around the room. There should be two of each symbol or picture. Suggestions: geometric shapes, apples, oranges, bananas, teddy bears, etc. Divide the children into teams and assign each team a base. The children hunt for the cards, bring them back to base and match them up. After a certain period of time teams are allowed to swap 1 for 1. The team collecting the highest number of pairs wins.

WIND UP 1

Refer to the Warm Up and Consolidation - matching pairs. Review the questions from the Warm Up.

WARM UP 2

Produce a series of cards containing things that friends do and are and things that friends do not do and are not. Suggested attributes include: Help each other, Dislike each other, Love each other, Are spiteful, Look after each other, Are jealous, etc. Pin up a card saying 'Friends' at the top of the board. Underneath have 2 columns, one with a tick at the top and the other with a cross at the top. Read out the statements about friends one at a time and ask the children to decide which side of the board to pin each one. Go over the characteristics of a friend. In today's true story from the Bible we will find out about two men who were great friends. Come back and tell me:

1. What were their names?

2. How did they show their friendship for each other?

CONSOLIDATION 2

Prepare a series of seven cards (page 38) containing the following pictures from the story: a moon, a wine goblet (represents a feast), a scroll (the covenant between David and Jonathan), a rock (to hide David), the figure 3 (3 arrows) a spear and a heart (friendship). You need one set for every two children. Scatter the cards randomly around the room. The children play in pairs and must hold hands throughout. If the children let go of each other they forfeit one of their cards, which is rescattered with the rest. The winning pair is the first to collect seven different cards.

WIND UP 2

Go over the attributes of friendship from the Warm Up. Review the questions. Talk about friends sticking together. Refer to the Consolidation and the need to hold hands if they were to succeed. Use the pictures to remind children of the main details of the story.

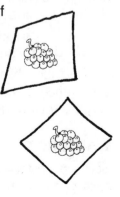

DAVID, CONFIDENT OF GOD'S SOVEREIGNTY

Text: Read and study 1 Samuel 26:1-25.

Teaching Point: David trusted God to do the right thing.

Lesson 17

WARM UP 1

Ask for volunteers who will trust you and do what you ask them. Give them tasks that seem difficult. Show them the task then blindfold them before they try it. Once they have been blindfolded make the task easier, e.g. • Go through a 'minefield' of paper cups - Remove the cups once blindfolded. • Run the Gauntlet - widen once the person is blindfolded and substitute balloons for batons. Today's true story from the Bible is about a man who was in a difficult situation. Should he sort it out himself, or should he leave it to God? Come back and tell me:

1. What was the name of the man?

2. What was the difficult situation?

3. What could he have done to sort it out?

4. Why didn't he do it?

CONSOLIDATION 1

The aim is to steal a spear and water jar without detection. The children stand in a circle with a blindfolded Saul in the middle. Saul lies down as though asleep. A paper spear and water jar are by his side. The leader indicates two children to creep in and try to steal the spear and water jar without Saul hearing. If Saul hears anything he shouts 'stop' and the two children freeze. If Saul can point at the children, the one he points to becomes Saul.

WIND UP 1

Remind the children of the Warm Up and the importance of trusting the leader to guide you aright. Review the questions.

WARM UP 2

Set up an obstacle course using easily moved items such as disposable cups, or crunchy items such as popadoms. Ask for a volunteer from the children. Show him the course before blindfolding him. Explain that two leaders will give instructions to guide him through the course, but one leader may give the wrong instructions. He must decide which instruction to follow each time. Leaders 1 and 2 give contrary instructions, e.g. 'take three steps forward,' and 'take four steps forward'. One leader should always give correct instructions. If the child reaches the end successfully, comment on him following leader 1's instructions, thus demonstrating trust in leader 1. If the child is unsuccessful, point out that listening to leader 2 led him astray. In today's true story from the Bible we will find out whether David trusted God enough to do what was right in a difficult situation. Come back and tell me:

1. What was the situation?

2. What was David tempted to do to get out of it?

3. What was the right thing to do?

CONSOLIDATION 2

Divide the children into teams. Set up a course for each team. The children take it in turns to be blindfolded and led along the course by a leader or another child. The team to get all its members to the far end of the course first wins. Any child that does not want to be blindfolded can act as a guide.

WIND UP 2

Remind the children about the Warm Up and review the questions. Comment on the importance of trusting the right person and refer to the game. Those who really trusted their guides would have run down the course. David knew that he could trust God to do the right thing.

DAVID LEARNS REVERENCE FOR GOD

Text: Read and study 2 Samuel 5:1-5; 6:1-19.

Teaching Point: What it means to fear God.

WARM UP 1

Before the children arrive place a table at the front with things stacked on it, such as a pile of books, some disposable cups, etc. Tell the children that someone has left this table in the way and you must move it before you start. Ask 2 leaders to help you. Tell them that you are a specialist furniture remover and you know the right way to move things. If they want to do it properly, without spilling anything, they must follow your instructions exactly. If the children suggest moving the items off the table first tell them that that is not necessary. Someone with your skills can overcome such trifling problems. Instruct the leaders how to hold the table, how to place their feet, etc. The movers pay very little attention to the instructions. The table rocks, the items teeter and eventually fall off. The supervisor is furious.

Acknowledge the disaster. Today's true story from the Bible is about moving something to a new place. Come back and tell me:

1. What was moved?

2. How was it moved?

3. How should it have been moved?

4. What happened when it was moved wrongly?

CONSOLIDATION 1

Divide the children into teams and divide each team in half. Half the team is at one end of the course and half at the other end. The object is to carry the 'ark' successfully from one end to the other. Each team is provided with a table tennis ball for the ark and some containers to carry it. The older children carry the ark on a tray, the younger ones in a shallow bowl. Each team member has to carry the ark to the other end of the course, without touching it with his or her hands or spilling it, and tip it into the next person's container. If the ark is touched or dropped, that person returns to the start and goes again. The winning team is the first one where each team member changes place.

WIND UP 1

Comment on there being a right way and a wrong way to move things, referring to the Warm Up and game. Review the questions from the Warm Up. God is holy and has set out the only way we can approach him - through the death of Jesus.

Lesson 18

33

DAVID LEARNS REVERENCE FOR GOD

Text: Read and study 2 Samuel 5:1-5; 6:1-19.

Teaching Point: What it means to fear God.

WARM UP 2

Leader 1 puts on a crown and tells the children that he is the king. He tells the children to stand up. They must obey the king. Do some warm up exercises. Then tell the children to stand to attention. The king is going to inspect his troops. Start going from child to child, telling them to stand up straight, etc. Whilst this is going on Leader 2 strolls over and slaps Leader 1 on the back, saying, 'Hello, mate. How are you doing?' Leader 1 reacts crossly. 'Take your hands off me. That is no way to approach a king.' Leader 1 carries on inspecting the troops. Leader 3 comes over and shakes Leader 1 warmly by the hand, saying, 'Good morning, your majesty. It's so good to meet you.' Leader 1 reacts as before, then turns to the children and says, 'Don't they know I'm the king?' Leader 4 comes over and bows down before the king. Leader 1 smiles. 'That's better. That's the right way to approach a king.' Then Leader 1 banishes Leaders 2 and 3 for showing disrespect. (If there are not enough leaders, use 1 leader to approach the king, changing hats or jackets each time to demonstrate being different people.)

Ask the children, 'Were any of those the right way to approach a king? How would you approach a king?' Today's true story from the Bible is about a man who did not approach a king in the right way. Come back and tell me:

1. Who was the man?

2. Who was the king? *(God)*

3. What did the man do that was wrong? *(Touched the ark)*

4. What should they have done? *(Carried the ark on their shoulders rather than on a cart.)*

CONSOLIDATION 2

Play Grandmother's footsteps. Place a series of hats in a line at the front. Tell the children that they have to move up the room to the row of hats, pick one and put it on. The first child to don a hat wins. But, they must not move when you are looking. To warn them you will shout, 'Uzzah!' as you turn round. Anyone caught moving has to start again at the beginning. Repeat as often as required.

WIND UP 2

Remind the children of the Warm Up and review the questions. God is holy and he says how we should approach him, just like the king did. If we disobey God we will be punished, like in the game, (having to start again), or like Uzzah being killed in the Bible story. God has told us that the only way that we can approach him is through the death of Jesus.

DAVID KEEPS HIS PROMISES

Text: Read and study 2 Samuel 9:1-13.

Teaching Point: The importance of keeping promises.

WARM UP 1

Show the children some bank notes and play paper money. Which would they like? Why? Show them that real bank notes have written on them: 'I promise to pay...' The Bank that makes this money always keeps its promise. Talk about why this is important. How would we manage if we could not trust the Bank to keep its promise? If you have a large collection of copper coins pass them around the children so that they can see how heavy they are. Would they like to only have metal money? It is so good that the promise on a bank note can be trusted. Today's true story from the Bible is about a promise. Come back and tell me:

1. Who made the promise?

2. Who did he make it to?

3. How did he keep his promise?

CONSOLIDATION 1

Inside some tins in the middle of the room place different promises, i.e. I promise to carry you to the other side of the room, I promise to give you a sweet, etc. The children stand in a circle and pass a ball around the circle to music. When the music stops, the child holding the ball selects a box and hands it to the leader. The leader states who should perform the activity. After this is done the music resumes. No child should have more than one go.

WIND UP 1

Talk about the importance of keeping promises, referring to the Warm Up and Consolidation. Review the questions from the Warm Up. We can trust God to always keep his promises.

WARM UP 2

A skit or puppets (see script on page 81). Toby and Trudy are talking about what they have been doing. Trudy is excited about a trip to the cinema that is coming up. Toby asks, what trip? Trudy reminds him that he promised to go with her some time ago. Toby tries to wriggle out of the promise. Eventually he admits that he has been invited to go to a football match on the same day. Keeping his promise to Trudy isn't convenient, but he will keep it at a later date. Toby goes off. Trudy is upset. Today's true story from the Bible is about keeping promises. Come back and tell me:

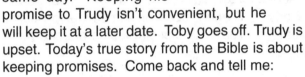

1. Who made the promise?

2. Who did he make it to?

3. How did he keep his promise?

CONSOLIDATION 2

Divide the children into teams. Each team sits one behind the other in a line. At one end of the line are a number of pieces of paper, rolled into tubes as scrolls. Write one word of the following sentence on eight of the pieces of paper: '*God can be trusted to keep his promises.*' At the other end of each line is the same number of table tennis balls as the total of pieces of paper. Each team send a scroll down the line and returns a table tennis ball. The scrolls are the message from David to Mephibosheth and the table tennis balls are Mephibosheth. Once all the scrolls and table tennis balls have changed ends the scrolls are opened and the eight words put into sentence order. The winning team is the first one to complete the exercise.

WIND UP 2

Remind the children about the Warm Up and review the questions. Point out that David kept his promise and sent for Mephibosheth, like in the game. God always keeps his promises and can be trusted.

SOLOMON'S WISDOM

Text: Read and study 1 Kings 3:3-28.

Teaching Point: God will equip his people to do his work.

WARM UP 1

Prepare a number of large pictures of people dressed in the clothes of their profession. Display them one by one to the children and ask them to guess what tools they need for their jobs. Hammer or nails for carpenter, paintbrush for painter, rake for a gardener, stethoscope for a doctor, Bible for a preacher, etc. Emphasise that special tools are needed for special jobs, e.g. a truck driver needs a driving licence, truck or something to deliver with, etc. Ask what special tool is needed for a King?

In today's true story from the Bible we will see what special tool the king asked for to help him be a good king. Come back and tell me:

1. What was the name of the king?

2. What did he ask for?

3. What did the tool help him do?

CONSOLIDATION 1

Demonstrate actions for each profession mentioned in the Warm Up, such as hammering a nail for the carpenter, driving a truck for the truck driver, etc. Include tapping forehead for wisdom for the king. Practise to allow the children to learn the actions. The game involves the leader calling out the name of one of the professions and the children performing the appropriate action. Anyone doing the wrong action goes to the 'Sin Bin' for a set number of turns.

WIND UP 1

People need the right tools for the job. What did Solomon need to do his job? How do we know God gave it to him? *(The story of the two women and the baby.)*

WARM UP 2

Divide the children into teams. The teams have to use their bodies to form the letters W, A, K, one after the other. Each time pin up the letter on a board. Explain what letters stand for: Wisdom - using the facts to make the right decision. And Knowledge acquiring facts. In today's true story from the Bible we will find out about someone who needed wisdom and knowledge. Come back and tell me:

1. What was the name of the person?

2. Why did he need wisdom and knowledge?

3. What did God give him as well?

CONSOLIDATION 2

Place a bucket of mixed cereals, pasta shapes, etc. in the centre. Divide the children into teams of no more than 6. Each team requires a cup or similar and a flat surface to sort on. The children take it in turns to run into the centre, scoop up a cupful of items and return to base. The children at base have to decide how to sort the items into different categories. At the end ask for feedback about which categories people sorted into. They could have sorted into big categories, e.g. cereal, pasta, pulses or into sub-sets, such as cornflakes, rice krispies, etc. All are valid. No one is wrong.

WIND UP 2

Go over the meaning of WAK. Refer to the Consolidation. They were not given instructions regarding the number of categories to sort into and they did not know how many different types of items there were. They needed wisdom and knowledge to sort it properly. Review the questions from the Warm Up.

Lesson 20

Diagramatic floor plan of the temple courts

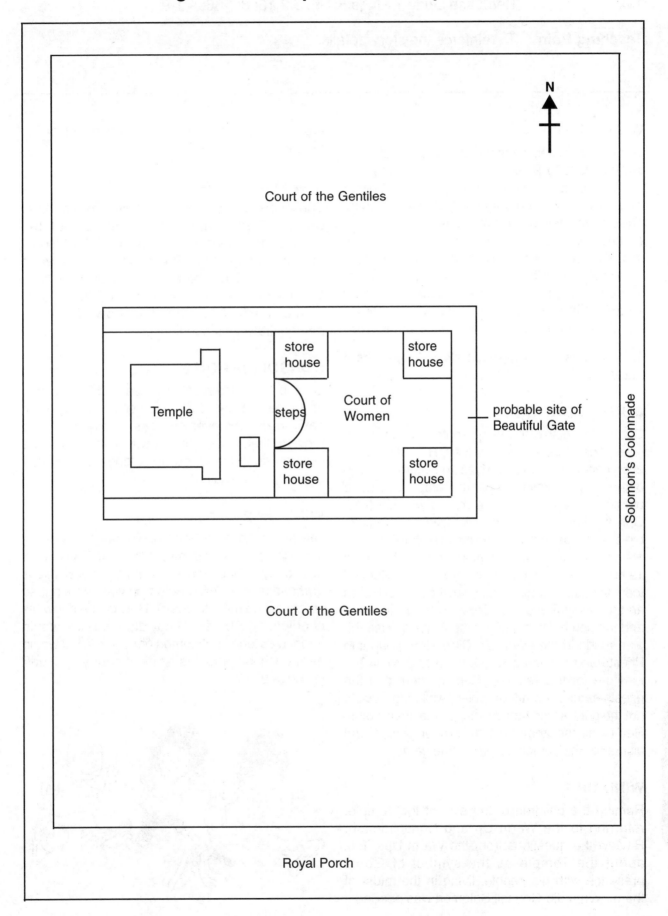

N

Court of the Gentiles

Temple

store house

store house

steps

Court of Women

store house

store house

probable site of Beautiful Gate

Solomon's Colonnade

Court of the Gentiles

Royal Porch

SOLOMON'S OBEDIENCE

Text: Read and study 1 Kings 5:1-6; 6:2-13; 8:1-66; 9:1-9.

Teaching Point: To reinforce the story details.

WARM UP 1

Using clotheslines, measure out the dimensions of the Temple (27 x 9 metres, with a porch at the front 4.5 m. deep and storerooms 2.3 m. wide on either side). Give some indication of the height - 13.5 m. The children help with the measuring and providing clotheslines in 9 and 18 m. lengths can facilitate this. If the room is not big enough, measure out an area half or one third of the size. Have a proper metre tape measure handy. Leave the marked out area for the Consolidation. Today's true story is about something this big. Come back and tell me:

1. What it is. 2. Who made it? 3. What was it made from?

CONSOLIDATION 1

Copy a floor plan of the Temple onto a transparency (see page 41) and put onto the OHP. Make sure everyone understands the size and internal design of the temple. Point out that the temple was not a big church where everyone met to worship God. Only the Priests and Levites went into the Temple, the ordinary people stayed in the courtyard. Provide objects for the children to make up a model of the Temple - cushions, cardboard boxes, etc. Remind them to make a partition between the Holy of Holies and the Holy Place, and between the Holy Place and the porch. Do not forget the 2 pillars. Use the plan made in the warm up. Divide the group into Priests and Levites and ask them to provide the furniture for the Temple. Remind them that the priests carried the ark on poles, while the Levites got the gold, silver, bronze, etc. for the storerooms. Return all the items to their proper places and dismantle the Temple as part of the game.

WIND UP 1

Remind the children of the size of the Temple, referring to the Warm Up and Consolidation. Review the questions from the Warm Up. Talk about the Temple as the symbol of God's presence with his people, living in the midst of them. What did God tell Solomon was needed if God was going to remain in the midst of his people? (1 Kings 9:4-9)

WARM UP 2

The leader acts as a keep fit instructor and asks the children to copy him. Talk about the importance of obedience. Refer to WAK (Wisdom and Knowledge) from the previous lesson Warm Up 2. Add an O for obedience. In today's true story from the Bible we see how obedient Solomon was. Come back and tell me how Solomon demonstrated his obedience.

CONSOLIDATION 2

Line up the children behind a leader. Put a crown on the leader's head for King Solomon. The children have to do whatever he does. Solomon walks forward, then flaps arms, crawls, jumps, etc. The children copy the leader in a long line. Change Solomons as required.

WIND UP 2

Talk about the importance of obedience, referring to the Warm Up and game. Who does God expect us to obey? *(God, the secular authorities, religious authorities, parents.)* Solomon was the king, so whom did he have to obey? How did he show his obedience to God? What did God say would happen as long as Solomon obeyed? What would happen if he and his sons disobeyed God? (1 Kings 9:4-9).

SOLOMON'S DISOBEDIENCE

Text: Read and study 1 Kings 11:1-43.

Teaching Point: The consequences of Solomon's disobedience.

WARM UP 1

Tell the children that you are a great athlete. Your coach tells you that you have to train hard. Go for a 5 mile run every day. Run on the spot and get the children to join in. Then you decide you have done enough. It's not 5 miles, but the coach won't know. You also have to swim a mile. Do swimming actions with the children joining in. After a short while give up. It wasn't a mile, but the coach won't know. You have to lift weights for 20 minutes. Ask the children to join in. Give up after a short time. The coach won't know. 'In fact, I don't really need to do any of it, do I? The coach won't know. Do you think I will still get the gold medal?' No!! Solomon started well, but in today's true story from the Bible he stopped doing what God said. Come back and tell me:

1. How did Solomon disobey?

2. What was the result?

CONSOLIDATION 1

To demonstrate the need to closely follow instructions in order to get something right. Sit everyone in a circle facing inwards. Tell the children that you have decided that there is a right way and a wrong way to do something. You will show them the right way and they are to copy it. As each person performs the action you say whether they have got it right or wrong. Once they know the secret they are not to tell anyone. They demonstrate their knowledge by getting it right when it is their turn. Hold a stick or pencil in the right hand and tap the floor with it rhythmically while saying, 'Tip, tap, tip, tap, do it this way.' Then pass the stick to the left-hand neighbour, using the left hand. The children will try and copy the rhythm and words, but these are unimportant. The secret is

using the right hand to tap and the left hand to pass the stick on.

WIND UP 1

Go back over the Warm Up and the need to keep on doing what is right. Review the Warm Up questions. Refer to the Consolidation and the importance of following instructions exactly.

WARM UP 2

Leader 1 performs various actions, asking the children to copy him. Leader 2, dressed like a child, disobeys each time. Leader 1 gets more and more cross. Eventually leader 2 is sent out. Disobedience has consequences. In today's true story from the Bible we will see what happened when Solomon stopped doing what God said. Come back and tell me:

1. How did Solomon disobey?

2. What was the result?

CONSOLIDATION 2

Divide the children into 2, 3 or 4 teams. Mark off an area approx. 2m. square in the middle of the room with masking tape. The teams start at base. If 2 teams they start opposite each other, if 3 teams they make a triangle, if 4 teams they start on the 4 sides of the square. Place a chair in the middle of the marked area. Team members take it in turns to run into the centre, clockwise around the chair and back to base. The second child runs once the first child has returned. All the teams run at the same time. Any child who steps outside the marked area is out and penalises their team. The first team to complete the course with all its members intact wins. If all teams lose members, the winning team is the one with most members at the end of the game.

WIND UP 2

Point out that disobedience has consequences, referring to the Warm Up and Consolidation. Review the questions from the Warm Up.

ELIJAH AND THE DROUGHT

Text: Read and study 1 Kings 17:1-16.

Teaching Point: The words of a true prophet come to pass.

WARM UP 1

Skit or puppets (see script on page 82-83). Toby and Trudy are at summer camp and remembering all the fun they had the previous year. Trudy and her friends have built a den, but she refuses to tell Toby where, because he and his friends wrecked it the previous year. Max enters. Toby thinks it is his great friend Percy. (Max and Percy are cousins and virtually identical.) Toby greets Max with enthusiasm. Then the real Percy comes in. Toby is flabbergasted. Both Percy and Max insist that he is Percy. How can Toby tell them apart? The children are asked to help, but cannot identify the real Percy. Toby decides to give them a test. Percy was there last year, but Max was not. Toby asks them both to tell him how they ruined Trudy's den the previous year. Max does not know, but Percy recounts how they did it. They now know who is the real Percy, because he was the one whose words were true.

In today's true story from the Bible we will find out if someone is a true prophet. Come back and tell me:

1. What was his name?

2. How did he show he was a true prophet?

CONSOLIDATION 1

Find the real person. Dress up three or four leaders or older children in the same jackets, hats or similar. Tell the children that only one of them is real. Ask the children to line up in front of the person they think is the real one. Only those who choose correctly will win. The real one will always be the one the leader stands behind when the children have made their choice. The leader must not move around once he has asked the children to choose. Once the children have made their choice tell them which line has made the right choice. The other three lines of children are out. Once the three losing groups of children have moved to the side, the leader moves to stand behind another suspect and asks the remaining children to choose again. Repeat until only one child remains. Tell the children between each change that there may be a new suspect, so they may have to change each time. The leader must stand directly behind his choice for that round.

Repeat the game two or three times if time allows, using different children as the four suspects. Ask the children if they have worked out how the real one was chosen each time? If not, explain it. The real one was the one who had the leader's authority behind him.

WIND UP 1

Talk about how we recognise a true prophet, referring to the Warm Up. Review the questions from the Warm Up. Point out that the reason the prophet's words come true is because has appointed him. He speaks on God's authority (refer to the Consolidation).

ELIJAH AND THE DROUGHT

Text: Read and study 1 Kings 17:1-16.

Teaching Point: The words of a true prophet come to pass.

WARM UP 2

Display the following items in no particular order. Real paper money, toy paper money, a leather belt, a plastic belt, a real piece of fruit, a plastic fruit, a pottery plate, a paper plate, etc. If you have access to a real fur coat and an artificial fur coat, use these as well because of their similarity to Elijah's dress (2 Kings 1:7-8). Ask the children if they can allocate the items to different groups. They may need help to identify that the groups are real and fake.

In today's true story from the Bible we will find out how to tell if someone is a true prophet. Come back and tell me:

1. What was his name?

2. How did he show he was a true prophet?

CONSOLIDATION 2

The children are given a variety of instructions (see below). When they obey them ravens, made from black socks with something edible inside, will be catapulted onto the floor area, landing on the children. All will get fed eventually. You need the following:

6-8 black socks containing a wrapped sweet or small piece of wrapped bread. Do not use boiled sweets because of the risk of choking.

6 tasks on cards

1. Wade across the brook and make like a rock.

2. Drink water from the brook.

3. Get out of bed and wash in the brook.

4. Run around the room then lie down.

5. Huddle together to hide from the king.

6. Do your morning exercises.

Pick a card at random and read it out. After the children have performed the action lob in the ravens. Pick another card and repeat. While the children are performing the action other leaders refill the ravens. Make sure every child has received a reward by the end of the game.

WIND UP 2

Refer to the Warm Up. Why is it important to be able to distinguish the real from the fake? Review the questions from the Warm Up. How did God look after Elijah? Refer to the game.

ELIJAH AND THE WIDOW'S SON

Text: Read and study 1 Kings 17:17-24.

Memory verse: The Lord alone is God. 1 Kings 18:39.

Teaching point: How God demonstrates that Elijah is a true prophet.

WARM UP 1

Introduce 3 people. Say that one was a goalkeeper for their college football team. How can we find out which was the real goalkeeper and who are false ones? Asking is not enough because the false ones have been told not to tell the truth. Perform a test. Shoot some footballs at them and see if they drop, miss or look uncomfortable. The one who performs the best is the goalkeeper. If you have no footballers on your leadership team use a different scenario. In today's true story from the Bible, God proves that Elijah is a true prophet. Come back and tell me how he does so.

CONSOLIDATION 1

The children stand around a parachute holding it by the edges. Throw a ball into the centre and tell them how many times they will bounce it before it comes off. Repeat several times. Ask them if you are a true prophet? Send the boys in to sit on the floor in the centre. The girls repeat the memory verse on the downswing of the parachute, one word each time. Repeat with the girls in the centre.

WIND UP 1

Remind the children of the Warm Up. Who was the goalkeeper? Review the question from the Warm Up. Did you demonstrate that you are a prophet during the Consolidation? How can you tell a true prophet? Recite the memory verse.

WARM UP 2

Tell the children that you are a great athlete. You throw a ball with pinpoint accuracy. To demonstrate you will throw a ball through a hoop. Try three times missing each time. Ask the children how you did. Well, you might not be the best ball thrower in the world, but you are the strongest. To demonstrate you will have a tug of war with the whole Sunday School and win. Line the children up in order of height with the smallest at the front. Take a tug of war rope and wrap one end around your waist. The children pick up the other end. On command, 'Pull!'

the children take the strain. Allow them to pull you over and drag you along the ground. Ask them how you did. Are you the best ball thrower in the world? Are you the strongest person? How do they know? Your words did not come true. In today's true story from the Bible, God proves that Elijah is a true prophet. Come back and tell me how he does so.

CONSOLIDATION 2

Divide the children into teams. Prepare 10 questions on the Bible story. Write out the memory verse on 10 pieces of paper and photocopy one set for each team, preferably on a different coloured paper for each team. Place the jumbled up words at one end of the room. Assign a leader to each team and give each one a set of questions. As the children answer the questions they run to the other end of the room and collect a word. The winning team is the first one to collect all their words and place them in the correct order.

WIND UP 2

Remind the children about the Warm Up and how we can tell a true prophet. How did God prove to the widow that Elijah was a true prophet? What was the most important thing that the widow could learn from Elijah? Repeat the memory verse. Learn it to 'The Farmer's in his den'.

> The Lord alone is God (x2) 1 Kings 18 verse 39,   The Lord alone is God.

ELIJAH AND THE PROPHETS OF BAAL

Text: Read and study 1 Kings 18:1-2,16-40.

Teaching Point: The Lord alone is God.

WARM UP 1

Tell the children that a prospective teacher, Mrs Imogen Arry is visiting today. You want the children to make her welcome, so that she will want to join the Sunday School. She has told you that she already knows some of the children. Enter Mrs I A. She goes up to one child as if she is the child's mother. (Prime the child beforehand.) She has been really worried because she couldn't find him. What time will he come home for lunch? etc. She does a similar routine with another child (previously primed). Then she purports to be the sister of a leader. The leader disagrees. Mrs I A leaves, telling her 'children' not to be late for lunch.

The leader explains that children have their own parents, not someone else's. The leader asks the two children their mother's name and establishes that Mrs I A was wrong. Mrs I A didn't seem to know her own mind.

Today's true story from the Bible is about people who did not know their own mind. They weren't sure whether the Lord was God, or someone else was God. Come back and tell me how God showed them he was the true God.

CONSOLIDATION 1

Devise various tasks for the children to perform. These can be places to go within the play area and things to do, such as take off shoes, put them back on, come here, go to the back, sit down over here, etc. Have plenty prepared. Ensure each command is not completed before issuing the next. Structure the commands so that there is plenty of running between different areas and chaos results. Call the children to order.

The Israelites were like this because they kept changing their minds about who was the true God.

WIND UP 1

Pick up on the difficulty the children had in the Consolidation. The Israelites were like this. They were unable to follow God properly because they sometimes followed Baal. Review the question from the Warm Up.

WARM UP 2

Display 3 or 4 objects on the table including a hinged box with a length of cotton thread or fishing line attached so that, with a pull from behind, the lid flies open. (This needs practice.) Hide a leader under the table holding the other end of the line. Leader 1 challenges the children to move the objects by ordering them to move one by one. Nothing happens. Leader 1 tells the children that they are obviously not shouting loudly enough. Repeat the process. Then Leader 1 commands the box to open and it does. Explain the trick. Magicians use tricks, but God doesn't. God performs miracles which really happen.

Today's true story from the Bible is about a miracle. Come back and tell me:

1. What was the miracle?

2. What did the miracle prove about God?

CONSOLIDATION 2

Tug of war. Divide the children into 2 sides so that their strengths are roughly equal. One side is the Lord and the other is Baal. Have two or three contests then reverse the names of the sides for a further 2 or 3. Leaders can help to ensure the sides evenly matched. Ensure the two sides win roughly turn and turn about. A commentator keeps everyone abreast of the action and remarks on first one side then the other side winning. Finish with 'The Lord' winning.

WIND UP 2

Remind the children of the Warm Up and review the questions. Remind the children of the tug of war consolidation. First the Lord's side won then Baal won. The Israelites were like that, first turning to Baal then to the Lord, then to Baal, then to the Lord. The Israelites needed to make up their mind. We need to make up our mind whether or not to follow God and stick with our decision.

ELIJAH HEARS GOD'S VOICE

Text: Read and study 1 Kings 18:41 - 19:18.

Teaching Point: God is in control, even when circumstances suggest otherwise.

WARM UP 1

The leader says that the children need to improve their spellings and maths. Use a board to do simple words and sums. Ask the children how to spell mat, cat, sat, etc. and simple sums such as 3+2, 2+2. The leader mishears and writes down wrong answers. Ask the children their names and mishear.

The leader explains that sometimes we do not listen or hear correctly, but God always does. Today's true story from the Bible is about God speaking to someone. Come back and tell me:

1. To whom did God speak?

2. How did God speak?

3. What did God say?

CONSOLIDATION 1

Quiz to review the Bible story (or series so far). Prepare the area as a game board. Divide the children into two teams. Each team has a line of three cages marked out on the floor (see diagram). (If you have a large number of children the younger ones can be the walls of the cages.) Inside each cage is a fierce animal (a younger child). The 2 teams start at the other end of the room from the quizmaster, one team behind each row of cages.

Prepare 16-18 questions. Divide each team into three groups. The first group stands by the first cage. They are asked a question. If they answer correctly they move on to the next cage. If they answer incorrectly the cage opens (the young children part) and the animal captures the children outside and brings them into the cage. Ask questions from each team alternately. Once the first group of children have either been caged or reached safety, the second group starts. Repeat with the third group. The winning team is the one that gets the most children to safety.

WIND UP 1

Remind the children of the Warm Up and the need to listen carefully if we are to get it right. Review the questions from the Warm Up.

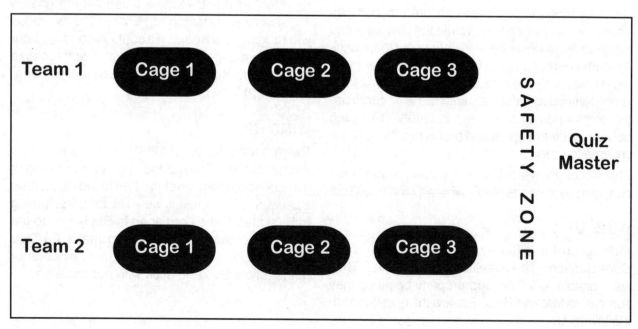

ELIJAH HEARS GOD'S VOICE

Text: Read and study 1 Kings 18:41 - 19:18.

Teaching Point: God is in control, even when circumstances suggest otherwise.

WARM UP 2

The issue is who is in control? A puppet or other leader challenges the authority of the leader by giving contradictory instructions.

Hide a puppet behind the leader but as close to the audience as possible so that it is clearly heard and seen. When the leader orders the children to stand up the puppet waits a second or so then appears suddenly and shouts, 'Sit down!' before disappearing. Some of the children will obey the puppet, some will not. The leader repeats the initial instruction. The puppet contradicts it. Continue, giving a variety of different instructions, such as run on the spot, touch your toes, touch your head (puppet says, 'Touch your toes.'), hop on one foot, etc. While this is going on the leader must reiterate that he is in charge, the children must do what he says. When the puppet pops up, the leader should ignore it initially, then look for it in wrong direction, finally becoming uneasy, frustrated and angry. Other leaders need to help the process by obeying the puppet if the children are slow to do so.

Point out to the children how confusing that was. Some of you obeyed me, some obeyed the puppet, and some didn't know whom to obey. We had total chaos. When we forget who is in control and stop trusting them, life gets very complicated and messy. In today's true story from the Bible we will learn what happened when someone forgot who was in control and tried to run away.

1. Who was the man?

2. Why did he run away?

3. Who did he forget was always in control?

CONSOLIDATION 2

Mark out four areas to represent wind, earthquake, fire and whisper. Mark each area with an appropriate picture or word so that the children can remember which is which. The children start in the centre. When you call out, 'Wind' all the children run to the appropriate location. Ask the children, 'Was God in the wind?' Shake your head. Call out all the other locations one at a time and ask the question each time, 'Was God in the ....?' To make the game more fun, call out a new name before all the children arrive at the first location. This will result in them running all over the place. Make sure they understand the rules and start off slowly before speeding the game up. The last child to the location could be declared out and removed from the game until a single winner is found. Repeat if interest remains high. Arrange it so that when all the children are in the 'whisper' location you speak softly and review the questions from the Warm Up.

To make the game more interesting the children can perform different actions at each location. Earthquake - shake, wind - shield face with arms as if fending off a blow, fire - make arms like flames above head, whisper - hand cupped to ear to listen.

WIND UP 2

Remind the children of the Warm Up and what happens when no one is in control. Review the questions from the Warm Up. God is always in control, everywhere and all the time. We can trust him to know everything that is happening to our friends and to us.

ELIJAH GETS A HELPER

Text: Read and study 1 Kings 19:19-21, 2 Kings 2:1-14.

Teaching point: God provides the right helper.

WARM UP 1

Ask the children to help get the room ready, put out the pens, glue, etc. Tell them you have been really busy, so arrived later than usual. Move some furniture on your own and fail. You need someone to help. Ask for volunteers. Today's true story from the Bible is about someone else who needed a helper. Come back and tell me:

1. Who needed a helper?

2. What was the name of the helper?

3. Why did he need a helper? *(To train him to take over as prophet after Elijah.)*

CONSOLIDATION 1

Back to back race (arms interlocked). Pair the children largest to smallest for maximum awkwardness. Medium sized children will do better. Say that many children found the race difficult because they did not have the right helper. Re-sort the children into similar sizes. Re-run the race. Say that it went much better because they had the right helpers.

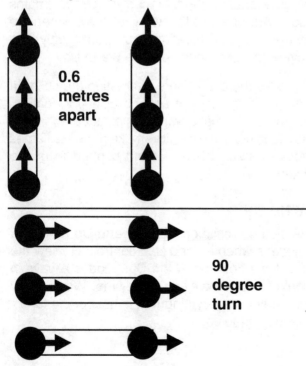

0.6 metres apart

90 degree turn

WIND UP 1

Remind the children of the Warm Up and your need for helpers. Refer to the Consolidation and comment on the importance of having the right helper. Review the questions from the Warm Up. God provided the right helper for Elijah.

WARM UP 2

Ask for 3 volunteers to build a plastic cup tower. Lets see who can build the tallest tower. Provide each volunteer with 20 plastic cups and a table to work on. It is possible to stack at least 15 disposable cups top to top and bottom to bottom before the tower starts to sway. Once the towers are as high as the volunteers can make them offer help from a leader. The taller person finds it easier to balance the cups properly. Point out the need for a helper. Today's true story from the Bible is about someone else who needed a helper.

Warm up Questions: See Warm Up 1

CONSOLIDATION 2

The older children form parallel lines with outstretched hands touching their neighbours' shoulders and legs apart. The lines are 0.6 metres apart (see diagram). On command, they make a ¼ turn to the right (practice this), so that the lines are at 90 degrees to the former lines. One younger child is the catcher. The other young children are hunted and have to stay inside the parallel lines. Every few seconds the leader gives the command to change. The children being hunted can only run down the lines and therefore change direction on each command. If children are caught they are 'dead' and drop out. The winner is the last child to remain free.

WIND UP 2

Review the warm up questions. Refer to the Consolidation and comment that the children had a good game and were out (dead) at just the right time. God's plan for our lives is perfect right up to the end.

GOD SAVES FROM SLAVERY

Text: Read and study 2 Kings 4:1-7.

Teaching Point: God cares for the poor and needy.

WARM UP 1

Place some clothes (garish jackets, shirts, hats, etc.) on a table. Tell the children that you owe some money and have to pay it back tomorrow. Reluctantly you have decided that the only thing to do is to sell some of your favourite clothes. Auction off the clothes having primed the leaders beforehand to 'buy' things. As the leaders buy the items they put them on. After the auction count up the money and discover that you still do not have sufficient to pay the debt. Ask the children what else can we do? How do they raise money at school? Talk about sponsored swims, walks, etc. Today's true story from the Bible is about someone who needed a lot of money and had nothing left to sell. Come back and tell me:

1. Why did she need the money?

2. How did God save her?

CONSOLIDATION 1

Divide the children into teams. Each team has a bucket full of table tennis balls (or pasta shapes, or scrunched up balls of paper) and some small containers. Place an empty bucket for each team at the far end of the room. The children take it in turns to fill the small container from the bucket and transfer the contents to the empty bucket. The first child to run returns to base before the next child goes. The first team to finish wins.

WIND UP 1

Remind the children of the Warm Up and how you raised the money. Review the questions. Use the Consolidatin to reinforce the details of filling the jars.

WARM UP 2

Use leader 2 as a slave. Leader 1, 'I've been shopping today and look what I've bought (point to leader 2). He's my slave. He has to do whatever I tell him.' Give the slave a series of tasks. After completing the tasks leader 2 asks for payment. Leader 1 refuses - 'No, I own you. You belong to me, you have to do what I tell you.' Leader 2, 'What happens if I say no?' Leader 1, 'I will beat you with my stick.' Ask the children, 'Would you like to be slaves? Do you think your parents would want to sell you to someone to be their slave?' In today's true story from the Bible a mother was told she had to sell her children to be slaves. Come back and tell me:

1. What was the name of the man God used to help her?

2. How did God help her?

CONSOLIDATION 2

If you have large numbers of children play this in teams, otherwise just as one group. Mark out an area for each group of slaves - the slave pen. Each slave pen has a leader as the slavemaster, who selects slaves to be freed. A small number of children start as freemen. Their job is to search for tokens or pretend money, which is hidden around the room. As soon as a token is found it is taken to the slavemaster, who frees one slave. That slave joins the searchers. If it is a team game the winner is the first team to free all the slaves. If the game needs to be extended make the searchers find two or three tokens to buy one slave.

WIND UP 2

Remind the children of the Warm Up and review the questions. Link in to the game. How did God show he cared for the poor woman and the boys?

GOD SAVES FROM DEATH

Text: Read and study 2 Kings 4:8-37.

Memory verse: Give thanks to the Lord for he is good. Psalm 107:1.

Teaching Point: God cares for the rich.

WARM UP 1

Who cares? Pin up pictures of a doctor, a nurse, a mother, and a lollipop man, asking the children to identify each one. (See page 40) Then show the following pictures to the children: sick man in hospital; baby; boy going to school; girl with grazed knee crying. Each time ask, 'Who cares for .....?' Match up the pictures. Some may have more than one answer. Ask who can remember the story about Elisha, the widow and her 2 sons? Who cared for the widow and her sons? *(God)* Does God care for ..... (each person in the picture)? God cares for everyone. In today's true story from the Bible we will hear about someone else that God cared for. Come back and tell me:

1. Who was it?

2. How did God care for that person?

CONSOLIDATION 1

The object is to reinforce the story details. Divide the children into teams. Prepare a set of 10 questions on the Bible story for each team. Write out the memory verse, one word on each piece of paper, and photocopy one set per team. Assign a leader to each team.   The leader asks the questions. As each question is answered, the child runs to the other end of the room and collects one piece of the memory verse. The leader asks the second question while the first child is collecting their piece. The first team to collect all their words and put the verse in order is the winner.

WIND UP 1

Remind the children of the series theme, God cares, referring to the Warm Up. Review the questions. God saved the poor woman's sons from slavery. God saved the rich woman's son from death. How does God save us?

WARM UP 2

On a table place a bottle of medicine (fruit drink or water with food colouring), a bottle of pills (Smarties), bandages, plasters and a sling. Tell the children that they are in a doctor's surgery and you need some volunteer doctors. Prime three leaders to be patients. The first is limping (hurt foot), the second has spots, and the third comes in and dies. The patients come in one at a time and each one is treated by two doctors, who have to decide what to use from the table to treat their patient. Change the doctors for each patient. At the end point out that you cannot treat someone who is dead. Today's true story from the Bible is about what happened when someone died. Come back and tell me: Who died? Who did God use to treat him? What treatment was used?

CONSOLIDATION 2

The children pretend to work in the field. Some children are designated as Elishas, but only the leader knows who they are. You need the same number of Elishas as teams. Start with teams of two. One child from each team runs to the field, picks an Elisha and brings him back to base. If the picked child is not Elisha he joins that team and another team member runs and chooses another Elisha. Continue until each team has found one Elisha. Repeat as often as required, changing Elishas each time.

WIND UP 2

What happened when Elisha was found? Review the Warm Up questions. God saved the woman's sons from slavery. God saved the rich woman's son from death. How does God save us?

GOD SAVES FROM DISEASE

Text: Read and study 2 Kings 5:1-19.

Teaching Point: To reinforce the story details / God cares for outsiders

---

WARM UP 1

Ask the children to perform the following actions: 7 hops; 7 runs on the spot; 7 sit ups; 7 roll side to side; 7 touch toes; 7 hold ankles and walk; 7 skips; 7 star jumps. Each time ask, 'Was that easy or hard?' In today's true story from the Bible someone had to do 7 things. Come back and tell me:

1. Who had to do 7 things and why?

2. What 7 things did he have to do?

3. Was it easy or hard for him?

4. What was the result?

CONSOLIDATION 1

This is like musical chairs. Designate 3 locations - a garage, a doctor's surgery and a teacher. Prepare a list of 12 problems, such as car broken down, sore throat, can't do my sums, flat tyre, hurt my leg, run out of petrol, bad tummy, flat battery, forgot my games kit, someone is bullying me, etc. The children move around to music. When the music stops, the children choose an area and run to it. Then the leader reads out the problem. The children in the correct area are the winners. Re-do as many times as required.

WIND UP 1

Remind the children of the Consolidation. Where do you go for help? Review the questions from the Warm Up. Where did Naaman go for help? Why didn't he go to the garage? The teacher? The doctor's surgery?

WARM UP 2

To teach what it means to be an outsider. Invite everyone present to join the club. Give it a name, such as Sunday Club. Make a big deal of being a member. It's only for us, etc. Leader 2 comes in from outside and asks, 'What are you doing?' 'We've formed a club.' 'Can I join?' 'No.' 'Why not?' etc. etc. Huddle in a circle and shout, 'Go away!' Leader 2 goes away looking sad. Talk to the children about being an outsider. Do you think God cares about people like that? Does God have a club that is only for some people, such as the good people? Today's true story from the Bible is about someone who was an outsider. Come back and tell me:

1. What was his name?

2. Why was he an outsider?

3. Who did he go to for help?

4. What was the result?

CONSOLIDATION 2

Designate three sites - Naaman's house, the Jordan river and Elisha's house. Demonstrate the following actions and ask the children to copy them: serving girl - sweep the floor; king's coming - stand up straight and salute; in the army - march on the spot; dip in the river – coopy down; leprosy - scratch arms and body; mules - get down on all fours. Once the children have mastered the commands, line them up in front of you in the centre of the room. Call out various actions and sites in random order. The children obey the command by performing the action or running to the appropriate site and back to the centre.

WIND UP 2

Remind the children of the Warm Up and review the questions. Refer to the game and obeying commands. What command did Naaman obey? Pick up on being an outsider. Naaman became an insider by being obedient.

GOD SAVES FROM STARVATION

Text: Read and study 2 Kings 6:24 - 7:16.

Memory verse: Give thanks to the Lord for he is good. Psalm 107:1.

Teaching point: God cares for his people.

WARM UP 1

Ask the children what they had for breakfast. What might I have had? For each suggestion reply, 'I would have liked ... for my breakfast, but when I went to the cupboard I found I'd run out.' Hold up an appropriate empty container. Suggested containers: cereal box, milk carton, butter dish, tea caddy, egg box, hot chocolate container, sugar bowl, etc. Ask the children what you can do about it *(go to the shops, borrow, etc.)* Tell the children that the shops were closed, your friends had run out too, etc. You are really, really hungry. Today's true story from the Bible is about some people who had run out of food. Come back and tell me:

1. Why had they run out of food?

2. What did God do about it?

CONSOLIDATION 1

Divide the children into teams and see who can collect the most food from the enemy's tent. Make a tent at one end of the room.(A sheet placed over the top of the chairs). The doorway should face away from the children. Place a large number of food items i.e. plastic food, empty containers, etc. inside the tent. The children take it in turns to crawl to the tent, enter, grab a piece of food and return to base. As soon as one child returns, the next one sets off. The winner is the team who collects the most food in a set period of time.

WIND UP 1

Who does God care for? the poor (widow & sons); the rich (woman of Shunam); the outsider (Naaman); his people (today) Recite memory verse.

WARM UP 2

Ask the children, 'What would happen if you had no food to eat? How would your tummy feel? Have you ever been really hungry? What happens if there is no food?' Points to bring out are: get thinner, sick, no energy, if you cut yourself it doesn't heal very well, die. Our bodies need food to stay healthy. Today's true story from the Bible is about some people who had run out of food. Come back and tell me:

1. Why had they run out of food?

2. What did God do about it?

CONSOLIDATION 2

Build a city from whatever is available - chairs, tables, sheets, etc. The city has to be big enough for everyone to get inside. Make four gates. Two leaders roam around outside as guards. The children try to get out of the city and go to the home base without being caught. The children in the home base are allowed to try to distract the guards. If caught, the child returns to the city.

WIND UP 2

Do the wind-up in the city. Remind the children of the Warm Up and review the questions. Who does God care for? the poor (widow & sons);the rich (woman of Shunam); the outsider (Naaman); his people (today) Recite the memory verse.

Lesson 31

DISREGARDING GOD'S WORD

Text: Read and study 2 Chronicles 17:1 - 19:3.

Teaching point: Listening to the wrong person leads to disaster.

WARM UP 1

This is designed to demonstrate the importance of listening to and following instructions. Dress up in an apron and chef's hat if you have one. Explain that you are a famous chef and about to make your special recipe. You need the children's help to make it. Place a simple recipe on the OHP or flip chart. On the table place the utensils and ingredients to make the recipe, some of which are not quite right, e.g. a plate instead of a mixing bowl, a whole onion instead of a peeled and chopped one. The children call out the ingredients and you follow their instructions, getting some of them wrong. Follow the same procedure as you make the recipe. Show the children the final result. Why hasn't the recipe worked? What went wrong?

In today's true story from the Bible we will learn about a king who did not do what he was told.

Come back and tell me:
1. What was his name?
2. Who did he listen to?
3. Who should he have listened to?

CONSOLIDATION 1

Mark out a course with various objects that have to be avoided. Blindfold 1-3 children at a time and ask them to traverse the course, by listening to instructions. Line up the remaining children on either side of the course. Tell the children that you will indicate which side is to give correct instructions and which side incorrect ones. The blindfolded children have to decide which side they will listen to. Children are eliminated once they have knocked over 3 obstacles. The children take turns to be blindfolded. At the start of each turn indicate which side is to give the correct instructions after the children have been blindfolded.

WIND UP 1

Talk about the game. What happened to those who did not follow instructions? Remind the children of the Warm Up. Did the chef listen to the instructions?

What was the result?

Review the questions from the Warm Up.

DISREGARDING GOD'S WORD

Text: Read and study 2 Chronicles 17:1 - 19:3.

Teaching point: Listening to the wrong person leads to disaster.

WARM UP 2

This is designed to demonstrate what can happen if you follow the instructions of someone who likes to do the wrong thing. Place a jug of water and some paper cups on a tray and cover the floor with a plastic tablecloth. Ask for a helper from among the leaders (or children). Explain that you have to prepare a tray full of drinks. Ask the helper to pour the drinks out. After the helper has poured out two drinks distract his attention, e.g. 'Hey, look what X is doing over there!' Then suggest he pour out one with eyes closed. Point out what happened when the helper followed the wrong instructions.

In today's true story from the Bible you will learn about a king who made the wrong friend. Come back and tell me:

1. What was his name?

2. Who did he make friends with?

3. Why was this friendship wrong?

CONSOLIDATION 2

The object is for the children to discover which leader can be trusted always to tell the truth. Place three leaders in different parts of the room and give each one a list of statements. One leader's statements are all true, the other two have some true and some false statements.

E.g.

Leader 1	There are 6 Bibles on the table by the door.
Leader 2	There are 9 Bibles on the table by the door.
Leader 3	There are 3 Bibles on the table by the door.

Other suggestions: someone's middle name is …….., the door in this room opens outward or inward, etc.

Divide the children into small groups of two or three. They approach the three leaders for a statement. They then check to see if the statement is correct. Carry on for a set period of time. At the end, the children line up in front of the leader they think is the reliable one.

WIND UP 2

Talk about the game. How did they decide who was the reliable leader? Remind them of what happened in the Warm Up and review the questions. Who should we listen to? Good friends suggest good things to do, wrong friends suggest bad things, so it matters whom we make our close friends.

LISTENING TO GOD'S WORD

Text: Read and study 2 Chronicles 20:1-30.

Teaching Point: The importance of going to God for help.

WARM UP 1

Leader 1 spills sugar or a similar substance on the floor. Help is needed to tidy it up. Someone gets the vacuum cleaner. Plug the cleaner into the power supply and switch on. Nothing happens. Can anyone help? I know nothing about electrical appliances. Leader 2 comes in. Checks that power is coming from the power point by plugging in another appliance, such as the OHP or a light to prove that there is power. Next, check the fuse in the cleaner. Leader 2 unscrews the back of the plug to discover that the fuse is missing. A fuse is produced and inserted into the plug and reassembled. The cleaner works. Demonstrate by cleaning up the sugar.

I couldn't fix the problem and I needed help from someone to do so. Today's true story from the Bible is about a man who had a very big problem. Come back and tell me:

1. Who had the problem?

2. What was the problem?

3. Whom did he go to for help?

CONSOLIDATION 1

Using part of 2 Chronicles 20:15, write out the letters of the following words onto coloured card or paper: *'The battle depends on God not on you.'* Write one letter on each piece of paper and colour code the paper so that each word is a different colour, e.g. the - blue, battle - yellow, etc. Hide the 29 letters around the room. Hang up a clothesline approximately 2 metres from the ground and provide 29 clothes pegs. Tell the children they are looking for laundry. Once they have found it they must separate it into colours, arrange the letters to make the word and peg them onto the clothesline. They are not allowed to stand on chairs. The only way to peg the words up is to ask the leaders for help. Then the leaders either peg the letters up or lift up the children for them to peg up the letters.

WIND UP 1

How did you get the letters onto the clothesline? How did you sort them into the right order? Could you have done it on your own? Remind them of the Warm Up and review the questions.

WARM UP 2

Ask for volunteers and give them tasks to perform that they cannot do without help, either from a leader or from other children. What do you need help with? Who do you ask for help?

Today's true story from the Bible is about a man who needed help. Come back and tell me:

1. Who had the problem?

2. What was the problem?

3. Whom did he go to for help?

CONSOLIDATION 2

Play a tagging game. Designate some leaders as catchers. The children try to evade capture. When caught, they must stand still with legs apart and shout for help. Another child crawls through their legs to release them.

WIND UP 2

Remind the children of the Warm Up and review the questions. Point out the importance of asking the right person for help. Link in to the game. Point out that they needed other children to release them after being captured. Jehoshaphat turned to God for help, not to his army.

OBEYING GOD'S WORD

Text: Read and study 2 Chronicles 34:1 - 35:19.

Teaching point: God's word is precious.

WARM UP 1

This is designed to interest the children in the details of the story. The book of the Law was found when they were looking for the money in the storeroom. Prepare a container with something unexpected inside it, such as a biscuit tin with a pencil inside or a rubber chicken. Ask for a volunteer. Tell the child to go out of the room while you hide the container. Ask him to come back in and find the container. The other children help by saying 'warm' or 'cold' as the finder gets closer or farther away from the container. When the container has been found ask the children what they think is inside it. Open it and show them what is there. Today's true story from the Bible is about a king who found something unexpected. Come back and tell me:

1. What was his name?

2. What was found?

CONSOLIDATION 1

Prepare a number of containers, at least one per child, by placing something inside each one. Some contain precious items, others ordinary items. The children hunt for the boxes. Once all have been found, open up the boxes in turn and see what is inside. The children decide whether the item is precious or not. Place the precious items on one table and the others on a different table. Talk about what makes each item precious. What was the precious thing God's people found in the story today?

WIND UP 1

Remind the children of the Warm Up and review the questions. Show them what Josiah found by showing them the appropriate part of the Old Testament. Most commentators suggest that it was all or part of Deuteronomy that was found, but some suggest it might have been the first five books of the Old Testament.

WARM UP 2

This is designed to demonstrate that the law was given so that we could enjoy our relationship with God and with each other. Prepare signs saying: No Singing, No Talking, No Noise, No sitting here, Enjoy Yourself, etc. Prior to the children's arrival place the signs in prominent positions around the room. Ask the children what they should do about the signs. Should they obey them? If not, why not? Ask which rules are good and why. In today's true story from the Bible you will learn about a king who found a book containing God's law.

1.   What was his name?

2.   What did he do about the book of the Law?

3.   What was the result?

CONSOLIDATION 2

Place A4 sheets of paper in a variety of colours all over the floor. You need at least one per child. The children move around to music. When the music stops they must stand on a sheet of paper. Those standing on a certain colour are the winners and get a point each. Change the winning colour at random. The children keep their own score. Reward everyone at the end of the game.

WIND UP 2

Talk about the game. Comment on their enjoyment. Remind them of the signs in the Warm Up. Review the questions from the Warm Up. Remind them that God gave his Law for our benefit.

SERVING GOD WITH PRAYER

Text: Read and study Nehemiah 1:1 - 2:10.

Teaching Point: We need to be concerned for God's honour.

WARM UP 1

Today we are going to start by doing something very important - speak to God. We know that he always listens when we talk to him. Pin up 3 pieces of card, one saying Thank You, one saying Sorry and one saying Asking. Ask who would like to pray. Ask what they want to say and point out if it is a thank you, sorry or asking prayer. Encourage children to have some of each type by asking, 'Does anybody want to say an asking prayer?' Be prepared to give suggestions for things to pray for.

In today's true story from the Bible a man prayed an asking prayer because he was very upset about something. Come back and tell me:

1. What was he upset about?

2. What did he want God to do?

CONSOLIDATION 1

The children make a boat out of tables and chairs on their sides (legs outwards). Covering them with a parachute or sheets gives a better effect. The boat must be big enough to contain all the children. (For a very large number of children you might need more than one boat.) Leader 1 gives a commentary about the increasing strength of the wind and waves. Other leaders spray the children with water in a plant sprayer. The boat begins to sink. The children have to decide what to do. Those who jump overboard get eaten by sharks.

Let them think about it for some time. Somewhere in the boat is a box or other piece of equipment labelled 'ships radio'. The only safe way out is to find the ship's radio and put out a distress call, asking for help. When they do this the leaders swarm in as lifeboat men and rescue the sailors.

WIND UP 1

With everyone in the boat. When we feel upset or are in trouble we should always ask God to help us. Sometimes we forget to and God is waiting for us to ask him for help. As soon as we do he is strong and powerful and will help us. Who was the person in the story who prayed for God to help him? What was he upset about? *(God's name was being dishonoured.)* Talk about how they feel when people at school swear and blaspheme. It's right to be upset. How did God answer Nehemiah's prayer?

SERVING GOD WITH PRAYER

Text: Read and study Nehemiah 1:1 - 2:10.

Teaching Point: We need to be concerned for God's honour.

WARM UP

Make a chart.

Item	Very important	Quite important	Not important
Friends			
Home			
Clothes			

Ask them to decide how important a variety of things are, such as friends, home, clothes, football, gardening, Head of State, Mickey Mouse, etc., ending with God. Most children will say that God is very important, in which case you can ask, 'How does it make you feel when people say God is not important?' If they do not say that God is very important tell them that Christians think God **is** very important - more important than anything else.

Today's true story from the Bible is about a man who thought God was very, very important and was very upset because lots of people were saying he was not important (tick not important box). Come back and tell me:

1. What was the name of the man?

2. Who did he go to for help?

CONSOLIDATION 2

Divide the children into teams. Hide small pieces of coloured paper, one colour per team and at least four pieces of paper per child. Write 'T' (which stands for trouble) on half of the papers. Give each team a leader and tell them which colour they are looking for. The children search for the papers. When they find a plain one they take it to their leader and continue searching. If they find one with T on it they have to stay where they are and shout for help until their leader comes to get the paper. The winning team is those with the most pieces of paper at the end of the game.

WIND UP 2

In the game when we came across trouble what did we do? *(Called for help.)* Review the questions from the Warm Up. What was Nehemiah's trouble? What did he do? Did God answer his prayer? Finish with prayer, thanking God for his promise to help us when we are in trouble.

SERVING GOD WITH HARD WORK

Text: Read and study Nehemiah 2:11 - 6:16.

Teaching Point: How to deal with opposition.

WARM UP 1

Leaders 1 and 2 must each build a tower out of paper cups. An enemy (Leader 3) tries to knock down the towers. One watches but does not build. One builds but does not watch. Neither makes any progress. In today's true story from the Bible someone is trying to build and someone is trying to destroy. Come back and tell me:

1. Who was trying to build?

2. What were they trying to build?

3. Who was trying to destroy it?

CONSOLIDATION 1

Give the children newspapers and ask them to cover the whole floor. While they are doing this two leaders mess it up in different ways, stealing the newspaper, scuffing it up and throwing it around. This should be done in brief raids. The children need to organise themselves to repel the raiders. They should be asked, 'What did Nehemiah do? How did he deal with this sort of thing?' Encourage them to post guards and some work while some deal with the raiders. Leaders must be responsible and allow themselves to be restrained. They must not mow down children in their excitement. They should run away rather than become involved in brawls.

WIND UP 1

Remind the children of the Warm Up and review the questions. How did they deal with opposition in the game? Was this how Nehemiah dealt with it? Discuss the opposition they face at school if the age of the children makes this appropriate.

WARM UP 2

In advance, write on large pieces of paper the things that happened to Nehemiah: tricks, temptation (to do wrong), lies (about him), traps, attacks (on the wall). Fold up the papers and put them in a bag. Tell the children that all the things in the bag are things that happened to Nehemiah. Ask for volunteers to come to the front and pick one out, read it or give it to the leader. Ask children if it was an easy or hard thing, good or bad. Continue until the bag is empty. In today's true story from the Bible we will see what Nehemiah did about all these hard things that happened to him. Listen carefully so that you can come back and tell me what he did.

CONSOLIDATION 2

Prepare a box of soft missiles, such as sponges or scrunched up balls of newspaper. Label the box 'Prayer'. Organise an attack (military operation). The children are to defend themselves against the leaders. They build themselves a fortress out of whatever is on hand, chairs, tables, etc. The leaders attack, dismantle the fortress and take the children into captivity. The children rebuild their fortress again. Once they are all inside, talk about Nehemiah and the opposition he faced. Tell them that what they need is a secret weapon, which they can have if they can guess what the Christian's secret weapon is. When they guess 'prayer' give them the ammunition box. The leaders attack again. A direct hit repels or kills a leader (depending on how many you have). The children are now easily able to defend themselves.

WIND UP 2

Have the wind-up in the fortress. Talk about Nehemiah's opposition and how he dealt with it. Talk about the opposition they face if the ages of the children make it appropriate. Finish by pointing out the importance of prayer.

SERVING GOD WITH GLADNESS

Text: Read and study Nehemiah 8:1-18; 12:27-43.

Teaching Point: I need to understand God's word if I am to serve him properly.

WARM UP 1

Leader 2 sits on a chair, gagged, with a small bag of sweets or fruit and a notice saying, 'If you please me you can have this.' The children come up and try to please him. No one can please him. Leader 1 points out how difficult it is to please this person because no one knows how. Leader 1 encourages the children to say that if the person could speak he could tell them how to please him and they could get the sweets. In today's true story from the Bible we see how God's people found out how they could please him.
Come back and tell me:

1. How did they find out?
2. What did they do to please God?

CONSOLIDATION 1

A treasure hunt. Divide the children into small groups. Prepare instructions to enable each group to visit 10 different locations. Start each group at a different location and send each on a different route.
Each instruction is in an envelope which is colour coded for each group. The group opens its envelope, and follows the instruction to get to their next location. When they get there they find their colour-coded envelope to get their next instruction. At the final destination their envelope contains their treasure (chocolate coins, lollies, etc.)

WIND UP 1

Remind the children about the Warm Up and how Leader 2 could not tell them how to please him because he could not speak. We only know how to please God because he tells us in his word, the Bible. The Bible is God's instructions on how to please him. We need to follow these instructions. Just as Ezra needed to read the book of the law so that they would UNDERSTAND and OBEY it, (Minister's name) reads and explains God's word to the grown ups so they can UNDERSTAND and OBEY it. The leaders in Sunday school read and explain God's word to you so that you can ... and ... it (get them to say the words).

WARM UP 2

Ask the children what sin is. Do you know that sin ruins things? Leader 1 takes a balloon and says, 'Sin ruins lives, just like this pin will ruin this balloon.' Leader 1 pops the balloon. You could point out different kinds of sin and pop more balloons. In today's true story from the Bible the people were sad about their sins, but discovered something wonderful. Come back and tell me what they discovered.

CONSOLIDATION 2

Cut the damaged balloons into enough pieces, one for each child. Hide them. Blow up enough balloons so that each child can have one attached to a string. The children find a piece of old balloon, take it to leader 1 and exchange it for a new balloon. Then he helps others find their pieces. When all have found their balloons ask:

1. What were God's people sad about?
2. What was the wonderful thing they discovered?

Just like you exchanged your damaged balloon for a new one, they found they could be forgiven by God and have a new start. They had a party, so we are going to have one now. Have music and serve drinks, biscuits and/or crisps.

WIND UP 2

Remind the children about the Warm Up and game. Point out the importance of understanding God's word if we are to obey it.

ESTHER CHOSEN AS QUEEN

Text: Read and study Esther 1:1 - 4:17.

Teaching point: God prepares a deliverer for his people.

WARM UP 1

Leader 2, dressed as a robber in a mask and cap, steals Leader 1's bag and runs out. Immediately a policeman (leader 2 wearing a helmet or with an ID card) comes in. Leader 1 is delighted to see the policeman and tells him about the robber. The policeman runs off and returns with the bag. He tells Leader 1 that he has arrested the robber. Leader 1 says, 'Wasn't that fortunate? I just needed a policeman and there one was.' Leader 1 pretends to choke. Leader 2 (or 3) jumps from the audience with stethoscope or 'Doctor' sticker and resuscitates leader 1. Leader 1 recovers and says, 'Thank you, I just needed a doctor and there he was.' In today's true story from the Bible someone was in the right place at the right time to help God's people. Come back and tell me:

1. Who was that person?

2. Why did God's people need help?

CONSOLIDATION 1

Divide the children into teams of 6-10, with a leader in charge of each. Leader 1 tells them he wants a specific person, such as the smallest person. Each team submits a person. The smallest gains a point for his team. You need about 12 different categories. Suggestions are: bluest (or brownest) eyes, darkest hair, smallest ears, longest tongue, biggest feet (shoes), most red on their clothes, smelliest sock. The team that gains the most points wins.

WIND UP 1

Remind the children of the Warm Up and review the questions. Refer to the game. People were chosen by each team because they were the one most likely to win (the best for the job). Why did Esther get chosen? *(So God could use her to rescue his people.)* Who chose her? *(The king, but also God.)*

WARM UP 2

You need a selection of props to enable the children to get ready for whatever you tell them. Today we're going to think about getting ready. Ask for a volunteer. Whisper to him what he is to get ready for. E.g. a party, swimming, playing in the snow, bed. He selects from the props things, which will make him ready, such as a swimming towel, goggles and swimsuit for swimming. The older children have to guess what he has got ready for. Then another child has a turn.

In today's true story from the Bible God is getting someone ready to do a special job. Come back and tell me:

1. Who was that person?

2.   What was the job?

CONSOLIDATION 2

Divide the children into groups, each with a leader. Give each group a different scenario to get ready for. Suggestions are: a visit by the Head of State, a flu epidemic, a school bazaar, Christmas or other festival. Give them whatever equipment you have, such as sweets, blankets, cushions, boxes, cups, buckets, rugs or carpet squares, toys. They can use the equipment creatively to set up their corner of the room. All the children visit all the sites and the children explain how they have got ready.

WIND UP 2

Talk about getting ready, referring to the Warm Up and game. Review the questions from the warm up, emphasising how God was getting Esther ready for a job.

ESTHER SAVES HER PEOPLE

Text: Read and study Esther 5:1 – 10:3.

Memory Verse: Leave all you worries with God, because he cares for you. 1 Peter 5:7

Teaching point: To teach that God overrules for good.

WARM UP 1

'Who wants to be a Millionaire?' format quiz. Use one child volunteer per question. If they do not know the answer they may ask the audience or use 50/50 (two wrong answers are removed).

Question 1: You find you have trodden in quicksand and are sinking fast. Do you:

  a) Try to shout for help? *(no)*

  b) Stand very still? *(no)*

  c) Lie down flat? *(yes - this stops you sinking faster)*

  d) Jump up and down? *(no - you will sink quicker)*

Question 2: You are walking in the woods and meet a bear. Do you:

  a) Climb a tree? *(no - bears climb trees)*

  b) Run away? *(no - bears run quicker)*

  c) Lie down? *(no)*

  d) Make yourself look bigger and make a loud noise? *(yes - not that successful but the best option.)*

In both these questions we have a dangerous situation and the right thing to do requires bravery. In today's true story from the Bible God's people were in great danger and Queen Esther needed to do a brave thing to save them.

  1. What was the danger?

  2. What was the brave thing?

CONSOLIDATION 1

Banquet game. Hide knives, forks, spoons, napkins, cups, plates, tablecloths (could be plastic or paper), enough for each child (+/- leaders). Tell the children to set up for a banquet. They need to erect a table, set it, find chairs, etc. and sit down ready to eat.

WIND UP 1

Sitting round the table, recap on the story. Ask what was the danger? What was the brave thing? How did God save his people? Serve drinks and biscuits sitting at the banqueting table.

WARM UP 2

Memory verse focus. Review the memory verse: *'Leave all your worries with God, because he cares for you. 1 Peter 5:7.* Ask the children what they worry about. You may need to make suggestions to get them started. E.g. Does anyone here worry about the dark? Does anyone here worry about not having friends? Does anyone here worry about starting school?

Is there anything else? Write down the worries on strips of paper and pin up. Ask, 'What does our memory verse say we should do with our worries?'

Get out a pillowcase with a label on marked 'GOD'. Ask how we give our worries to God *(through prayer)*. Pray for each of the worries one by one and put them in the sack.

In today's true story from the Bible God's people are worried because something bad is going to happen to them. Do you think God is going to look after them? Come back and tell me:

  1. What was their worry?

  2. How did God care for them?

CONSOLIDATION 2

The oldest children, in pairs, are finders. All the other children have one word of the memory verse put on their backs (sticky labels are the easiest). They roam or hide wherever they like. The finders have to find and assemble the memory verse, i.e. round up a selection of smaller children in their home area. If left unguarded the children may escape or be stolen by other teams. The winning team is the first to get a group of children lined up displaying the memory verse on their backs.

WIND UP 2

Recap on the way God showed his care for the Jews and how he was working. Review the questions from the Warm Up. Point out God's control of events - Esther being made queen, Mordecai discovering the plot, the King receiving Esther, the Jews able to fight off those oppressing them. Recite the memory verse.

JOB

Text: Read and study Job 1:1 – 2:10; 42:10-17.

Teaching point: To understand that God is in control of every aspect of our lives and can be trusted.

WARM UP 1

Skit or puppets (see script on page 84). Toby tells the children about the terrible things that have happened to him, such as the goldfish dying, getting his finger shut in the door, losing his homework and the cat being sick in his bed. Trudy comes in and Toby tells her about it. Trudy commiserates with him. Toby cannot understand why all these dreadful things have happened. Trudy tries to explain it, using various superstitions like getting out of bed on the wrong side, walking under a ladder and breaking a mirror. Toby refutes each suggestion. Finally Toby suggests that maybe God does not love him anymore. When asked why, says because he is bad sometimes. Trudy points out that God's love does not depend on Toby being good. Toby feels better about things.

In today's true story from the Bible a man has lots of bad things happen to him and he doesn't know why. Come back and tell me:

1. What was the man's name?

2. What happened to him?

3. Why did it happen?

4. What was the result?

CONSOLIDATION 1

Place the following on a tray: a man, a woman, a boy, a girl, three men (ideally wearing different colours), a sheep, a cow, a camel (if possible), a donkey or horse. Ideally use plastic figures from a child's toybox. You could also use pictures. Ask the children to look at them. Cover the tray with a cloth and remove one secretly. Show the children the tray and see if they can tell you what is missing. The winner gets to remove one of the figures for the next go. For very large groups you may want to split the children and have more than one tray. It is difficult for more than 15-20 children to see the objects.

WIND UP 1

Review the questions from the Warm Up. Using the tray, talk about what Job had taken away - sons, daughters, camels, donkeys, sheep, cattle. Remove these from the tray as the children mention them. You will have the following left:

Job: What happened to Job? *(became ill)*

Woman: What did his wife tell him to do? *(curse God and die)*

Three men: What did his friends tell him? *(you must have done wrong)*

What did God say about it? *(The friends were wrong.)* Take them away.

What happened in the end? Replace the objects on the tray as the children tell you how Job's fortunes were restored.

JOB

Text: Read and study Job 1:1 – 2:10; 42:10-17.

Teaching point: To understand that God is in control of every aspect of our lives and can be trusted.

WARM UP 2

Prepare a photo album of about six things or people who are precious to you, such as children, parents, nieces or nephews, cat, etc. Talk about how precious they are as you tell the children about them, showing them the pictures. For larger groups the pictures can be reproduced on OHP transparencies for the OHP rather than in an album.

In today's true story from the Bible there is a man who has lots and lots of precious things. Come back and tell me:

1. What was the man's name?

2. What happened to his precious things?

3. Why did it happen?

4. What happened in the end?

CONSOLIDATION 2

The children move around to music. The leader stands with his back to the action. When the music stops the children choose to be a son or daughter - by standing straight, a cow, sheep, donkey or camel - by getting down on all fours, or Job - by lying down. The leader, who is not looking, calls out, 'Job's sons and daughters were taken away,' or 'Job's animals were taken away,' or 'Job became sick.' The children who have adopted the posture that goes with the call are out. Carry on until there is one winner. Repeat as often as required.

WIND UP 2

Review the questions from the Warm Up. After the third question remind the children that Job said, 'God is good'. Pin up a piece of card saying this. Job's wife, when she saw how much Job suffered, said, 'God is bad'. Pin up a card with this on it. But Job said, 'No, God is good.' Point to the first card. Job's friends, when they saw how much Job suffered, said 'Job is bad.' Pin up a card. But they were wrong. Take down 'Job is bad' and 'God is bad' cards. Review the fourth question from the Warm Up. God showed that Job was good by giving him back all the things which had been taken away.

OPPOSING GOD'S WORD

Text: Read and study Jeremiah 36:1-32.

Teaching point: The consequences of refusing to heed God's word.

WARM UP 1

Prepare two parcels appropriately gift wrapped and labelled. One label says, *Happy Birthday from Auntie ....*, and the other says, *Happy Christmas from Auntie ....* . On the back of both labels is written, *Do not open early otherwise terrible things will happen.* The Christmas present (parcel B) contains four pieces of card with the following words, *Jeremiah, Baruch, Jehoiakim, Jerusalem.* The birthday present (parcel A) contains an inflated balloon containing talcum powder. Show the children the parcels. Tell them that your aunt always likes to be in plenty of time, so she has sent you these presents early. Read out the labels. Your birthday is before Christmas, but it is still some time away. You have been looking at the parcels all week and you do not think you can wait until your birthday. Ask whether you should open parcel A. You do not really believe that your aunt would do something terrible. Open the parcel, using sharp scissors. Show the children the balloon, still holding the scissors. Point out that nothing terrible has happened. While talking to the children 'accidentally' burst the balloon with the scissors. Repeat the procedure with parcel B. Read out the words on the cards.

In today's true story from the Bible you will learn about a king who ignored instructions. What do the 4 words have to do with today's story?

CONSOLIDATION 1

Prepare a number of small scrolls, by cutting a sheet of A4 paper into eight pieces. You need about 20 scrolls for each team and each team's scrolls should be a different colour. On each piece of paper write, *Jeremiah 36:31.* Prior to the session hide the scrolls around the room. Divide the children into teams and allocate a colour to each team. Give the teams a set time limit to search for their scrolls. At the end of the time sit the children in a circle and place a bin in the centre of the room to be the fire. The children open their

scrolls and read out what is on them. Ask the children what King Jehoiakim did to God's word? Tell the children to throw the scrolls into the 'fire'. Point out that you have got rid of God's word. Prime a leader to say that there is still one left. The leader brings out a scroll, opens it up and reads out the reference. Read out the Bible verse. Point out to the children that Jehoiakim thought he had destroyed God's word, but God told Jeremiah to dictate it again.

WIND UP 1

Remind the children of what happened when instructions were ignored and the parcel was opened. Go over the four clues. Jehoiakim thought he could ignore God's word without anything bad happening. But he was wrong. The Bible tells us that the king of Babylon invaded Judah, captured Jehoiakim and took him back to Babylon in chains.

OPPOSING GOD'S WORD

Text: Read and study Jeremiah 36:1-32.

Teaching point: The consequences of refusing to heed God's word.

WARM UP 2

Leader 1, dressed as a headteacher if possible, enters and introduces himself. 'I am ……….. and I am the Headteacher of …….. school. I have a very naughty pupil. I keep writing to his parents to tell them bad things will happen if his behaviour doesn't improve, but I don't think they get them. So I've written another one (reads out a short letter). I've got 10 copies. There are 10 envelopes in this room. Can you find them and put a letter in each?' The children search for the envelopes. When found the headmaster gives the finders a letter to put in each envelope. The child who found and stuffed the envelope holds on to it. 'I want you to make sure he doesn't lose it this time, so if he does you give him another one.'

Leader 1 calls in Leader 2, who is dressed as a schoolboy with tie under one ear. He gives him a dressing down, then gives him an envelope to take home to his parents. Leader 2 immediately drops it. Ask a child to give him another. Leader 2 puts it in the bin. He is given another and tears it up. He is given another. (By this stage he is likely to be surrounded by children with letters). Leader 2 says, 'OK, I get the message.'

Today's true story from the Bible is about someone who doesn't want to get a message.

Come back and tell me:

1. What was his name?

2. Who sent him the message?

3. What did he do with the message?

CONSOLIDATION 2

A message sending game. The children sit in a circle holding hands. One person says, 'I'm going to send a message to …(e.g. Sarah) and squeezes a hand beside her. The next person passes on the squeeze until the squeeze reaches Sarah. She says, 'I've got the message' and decides whom to send one to next. She may send the squeeze in either direction, but not in both. Once the children have got the hang of this, you can have someone in the middle of the circle trying to detect the message in transit. If they do, they change places with the one who has been caught.

WIND UP 2

Show a few things which will send messages, such as a pager or mobile phone, a birthday card, a torch for Morse code. Review the questions from the Warm Up. Do you think that what the king did was a wise or a foolish thing for him to do? Why?

UNDECIDED ABOUT GOD'S WORD

Text: Read and study Jeremiah 37:1 - 39:18.

Teaching Point: Listening to God's word is no good unless it is obeyed.

WARM UP 1

Skit or puppets (see script on page 85). Toby and Trudy give conflicting advice about three or four different coloured buckets on the table. In a hat somewhere in the room is a soft toy. The leader asks if anyone has seen the soft toy? Toby and Trudy argue about where the soft toy is hiding. Trudy says it is under one of the buckets. Toby says it is in the hat. The leader asks the children which one he should believe? He looks under the bucket suggested by Trudy. When the bucket is found to be empty, Trudy says she made a mistake. The soft toy is really under a different bucket. The leader looks under that bucket. Trudy says the soft toy is really under a third bucket. The leader asks the children if he should believe what Trudy says? He looks under the third bucket to no avail. The leader says that he thinks he has been listening to the wrong person. He asks Toby where the soft toy is. Toby says that the soft toy is in the hat. The leader looks in the hat and finds the soft toy.

Today's true story from the Bible is about a man who couldn't make up his mind who to listen to. Come back and tell me:

1.   What was the name of the man?
2.   Who gave him good advice?
3.   Who gave him bad advice?
4.   Whom did he listen to?

CONSOLIDATION 1

A quiz. Divide the children into two teams. Prepare a set of questions on the Bible story. Ask the questions of each team alternately. If the answer is correct, a team member chooses a plastic mug and takes it back to their team. Inside is a piece of paper with a score of 1-4 which tells them how many points they have got for their answer. The winning team is the one with the most points at the end of the quiz.

WIND UP 1

Remind the children of the Warm Up and review the questions. Point out the consequences of Zedekiah listening to the wrong people.

WARM UP 2

Place five items under five buckets (or smaller items under plastic cups), preferably different colours. Leader 1 lifts each bucket to show what is there, then hides his eyes or leaves the room whilst a child or children mix them up. Leader 1 returns and states which item they are looking for and asks the children where it is. Leader 2 leads a chorus of conflicting advice. Leader 1 tries to find out who is telling the truth. He asks whom he can believe. In the end he disregards all the advice and chooses another bucket.

Today's true story from the Bible is about a king who cannot decide whom to listen to. Come back and tell me:

1.   What was the name of the king?
2.   Who gave him good advice?
3.   Who gave him bad advice?
4.   Whom did he listen to?

CONSOLIDATION 2

Label areas in the room north, south, east and west according to the compass. The children have to decide where to go. Several leaders direct the children. One leader always gives good advice. The others give a mixture of good and bad. The right places to go follow the N E W S pattern. The children have to work out whom to trust, or else the right order in which to visit the places. After each go tell the children which group is right. No children need be out. Carry on until most children know where to go each time.

WIND UP 2

Remind the children about the Warm Up and review the questions. Point out the importance of listening to the right person, with reference to the game.

GOD SAVES FROM DEFILEMENT

Text: Read and study Daniel 1:1-21.

Teaching Point: The importance of putting God first.

WARM UP 1

Invite about three children and one leader to the front. Say you are looking for a new servant. Look at their height, age, muscles. Give them a task to do, such as setting a table, with tea towel over arm, then pouring a drink from a jug to a beaker. Leader 2 does it all wrong and plays for laughs. Today's true story from the Bible is about some of God's people who were chosen for a special job, but were asked to do something they knew God would not be pleased with. Come back and tell me:

1. Who they were?

2. What were they asked to do?

CONSOLIDATION 1

A quiz to reinforce the story detail. Divide the children into teams of not more than 10. Each team has to try and reach safety by crossing over five stepping stones. Each question answered correctly allows someone to step onto a stepping-stone. First correct answer, child 1 steps onto the first stone. Second correct answer, child 1 moves to the second stone and child 2 steps onto the first stone, etc. Continue until the whole team is across. You will need at least five more questions than the number in the team. This game is better if all teams have their own leader to ask the questions of their team. It could be played with 1 question master if there are no more than two teams, but you would need double the number of questions.

WIND UP 1

Remind the children about the Warm Up and review the questions. What did Daniel and his friends do about the food and drink? Every day when they ate different food they would be reminded that they were God's people and he had to come first.

WARM UP 2

Odd ones out. Show the children several collections of 4-5 small objects, one of which is an odd one out. Suggested items: things made of wood + 1 plastic, 4 animals + 1 non-animal, coins + 1 foreign, 3 things used for cooking + 1 non-edible. Ask if any of them have ever felt the odd one out. Most of them will have, particularly if they have a Christian background. Ask whether they liked it. Today's true story from the Bible is about some young men who were the odd ones out and wanted to be. Come back and tell me:

1. Why were they the odd ones out?

2. Why did they want to be?

CONSOLIDATION 2

Children are in teams, sitting in a row facing forward. Each team has a pile of vegetables of different shapes and sizes at the end of the row. Also an empty basket, bucket or container at the same end as the pile of vegetables. The children have to pass the vegetables from one to another as fast as they can. When the vegetable gets to the end of the row they have to pass it behind their backs until it gets back to the top and is placed in the basket. If the vegetable is dropped behind the back, no looking is allowed. The vegetable must be found by feel. Any number of vegetables can be in transit at any one time. The winner is the first team to get all their vegetables in the basket.

WIND UP 2

Remind the children about the Warm Up and review the questions. Every day when they ate different food they would be reminded that they were God's people and he had to come first.

GOD SAVES FROM EXECUTION

Text: Read and study Daniel 2:1-49.

Teaching point: God is in control of events.

WARM UP 1

The leader tells the children that he can read minds. A child volunteer comes out and is told to concentrate hard on something in their mind. The leader pretends to be concentrating hard and draws a non-specific shape, such as a triangle, square or circle, on a board so that the children can see. Ask the child what they were thinking and the leader pretends their drawing has something to do with it. Repeat as required. Ask the children if they think that you can really read minds? No, if there is any doubt. In today's true story from the Bible we find someone who really did know what someone else was thinking. Come back and tell me:

1. Who was it who knew what someone else was thinking?

2. Whose mind could he read?

3. Why was it important that he could do this?

CONSOLIDATION 1

Make a statue out of paper for each child. Make heads from gold paper, chest/arms from silver paper, thighs from bronze paper, legs from grey paper and feet from brown paper. Scatter the bits of the statues over a wide area, some can be hard to find. The children, in teams, find the pieces and bring them back to a home base as soon as they find them. Some children stay at the home base and assemble the statues by gluing them onto a large sheet of paper or newspaper. The winner is the team who assembles the most complete statues. Teams can swap pieces if they both agree to this.

WIND UP 1

Remind the children about the Warm Up and your inability to read minds. Review the questions. Ask the children what the statue was made from, referring to the Consolidation. How many rocks did it take to knock down the statue? God's kingdom is more powerful than all the rest.

WARM UP 2

Bring in objects made of gold (or gold-coloured), silver, bronze, iron or steel, clay and a big rock. Talk about each of these items as well as sports medals, such as Olympic medals. Which metal is the most valuable? What are the different uses? Point out the strengths, e.g. Iron and steel can be used for making bridges, etc. because they are very strong. Clay can be broken because it is not as strong. All of these things are in today's true story from the Bible. Come back and tell me how.

CONSOLIDATION 2

Small teams make statues out of anything on hand, such as plastic cups, empty drink bottles, sellotape, cans, drinking straws, wooden blocks, duplo or stickle bricks. Each team can have different materials; they do not have to be the same. Once the statues are finished, the children scrunch up three-four sheets of newspaper each for rocks, stand back and pelt the statues with them until they fall down. If time permits, groups can move round to have a go at building a statue out of different materials.

WIND UP 2

Go through each coloured item used in the warm up to recap on the story. Ask how many 'rocks' it took to knock our small statues down and how many rocks it took to knock down the one in the dream. God's kingdom is more powerful than all the rest.

GOD SAVES FROM THE FIERY FURNACE

Text: Read and study Daniel 3:1-30.

Teaching point: The need to trust God, even in difficult situations.

WARM UP 1

The object is to demonstrate what happens when things burn. You need a candle in a secure holder, a bowl of water, tongs, paper, marshmallows, 2 or 3 human hairs and a small piece of thinly cut ham. Talk about what happens when things burn. What is happening to the candle? Hold a marshmallow in the flame and watch it melt like the candle. Hold a piece of paper in the flame and demonstrate what happens. Is it black, fragile and small? Hold the hairs in the flame. These smell horrible as they burn. Comment on the smell. Hold the ham in the flame. Comment on the smell and how the fire changes and damages it.

Today's true story from the Bible is about a fire. Come back and tell me:

1. Who are the three men in the story?

2. What was strange about the fire?

CONSOLIDATION 1

Play 'Simon Says', but instead of 'Simon' use 'Nebuchadnezzar' says. All those who are out have to go into a pen made of chairs or tables and referred to as the fiery furnace.

WIND UP 1

Remind the children about the Warm Up and review the questions. Why didn't the fire burn Shadrach, Meshach and Abednego? Who was in control - Nebuchadnezzar or God? We can trust God to do what is right, even in difficult situations.

WARM UP 2

Ask for a volunteer to peel a banana. Separate the skin from the fruit. The leader slices the banana into small blocks. Ask another volunteer to tear a cereal box into as many pieces as possible. Place the bits in a pile. Ask a third volunteer to remove as many pages from an old telephone directory as possible. Separate the torn pages from the cover. Ask three more volunteers to reassemble all the items back to their original state. Give the volunteers two minutes to try. Can it be done? Why not? It is impossible. The banana is particularly difficult. In today's true story from the Bible we find God doing something which is completely impossible. Come back and tell me:

1. Who are the three men in the story?

2. What was the impossible thing that God did?

CONSOLIDATION 2

This story especially lends itself to drama. The leader reads the story. Choose Nebuchadnezzar, Shadrach, Meshach, Abednego, the Angel, guards and informers before you start. Build a pen of chairs for the fiery furnace and a stack of chairs, or other suitable object, for the statue. Let the children find their way along as you read the story with a few basic instructions.

Drama often feels chaotic but children enjoy it very much and learn a surprising amount through it.

WIND UP 2

Remind the children about the Warm Up and review the questions. Why didn't the fire burn Shadrach, Meshach and Abednego? Who was in control - Nebuchadnezzar or God? We can trust God to do what is right, even in difficult situations.

GOD SAVES FROM THE LIONS

Text: Read and study Daniel 6:1-28.

Teaching Point: The importance of trusting God for salvation.

WARM UP 1

Have a leader or willing older child at the front and tell the children we must ensure he does not escape. The children make suggestions about how to restrain him, such as tie up, blindfold, tie to a chair, post guards, etc. See if he can escape. Ask the children if they have done a good job.

Today's true story from the Bible is about a person in an impossible situation with no hope of rescue. Come back and tell me:

1. What was the person's name?

2. What was the impossible situation?

3. How did he escape?

CONSOLIDATION 1

Island rescue game. Use plastic sledges or prepare robust laundry baskets with bottom, front and back covered in cardboard. With reasonably small children you can use fruit and vegetable boxes found in supermarkets. They will not last as long but will do the job. You need one for each team. You also need a ball of string and two pieces of rope or washing line for each team.

All but the two largest of each team go and stand in an area of the room which is referred to as the island. It could be marked with a sheet or parachute. Each team could have their own small island or all could stand on one big one. The older children have all the equipment. They have to work out how to

rescue all the children from the island without going in the sea.

The idea is that they unravel some of the string and throw the ball to those to be rescued. Then tie on a piece of rope to the string and the other end of the rope to the box or basket. The second bit of rope is attached to the other side of the basket. The basket can now be hauled across to the island, pick up a child and hauled to safety. The winning team is the one who gets all their team to safety first.

Children will need some prompting to get started, but once they have the idea they will be able to get on with the game on their own.

WIND UP 1

Remind the children about the Warm Up and game. Review the questions from the Warm Up. Was Daniel able to organise his own escape? No, he had to trust God for his salvation.

GOD SAVES FROM THE LIONS

Text: Read and study Daniel 6:1-28.

Teaching Point: God can do the impossible.

WARM UP 2

Do some tricks. Place a bead (check it floats!) in a milk bottle and ask a child how to get it out without touching the bottle. Let some have a try. You can do it by filling the bottle with water until the bead floats to the top.

Ask the children how you can step through a small piece of paper (A4 or A5). Fold the paper in half and cut as per diagram. When unfolded this should make a loop of paper which can be easily stepped through.

Say, 'These are not magic, they are just tricks.'

In today's true story from the Bible something seemingly impossible happened, but it was no trick. Come back and tell me:

1. What was the person's name?

2. What was the situation?

3. What happened that seemed impossible?

CONSOLIDATION 2

Use sites and actions from the Daniel series. Designate four sites - fiery furnace, Judah, Babylon and the Lion's Den. Demonstrate the following actions and ask the children to copy them:

statue - stand up straight and keep still

vegetables - putting food in mouth and chewing

Daniel - on knees praying

Shadrach, Meshach and Abednego - form groups of three

rock - curl up

lions - get down on all fours.

Once the children have mastered the commands, line them up in front of you in the centre of the room. Call out various actions and sites in random order. The children obey the command by performing the action or running to the appropriate site and back to the centre.

WIND UP 2

Review the questions from the Warm Up. Show pictures of vegetables, the statue in the dream, the fiery furnace, and lions in the den. Ask how in each Daniel and his friends showed faithfulness to God and how God showed he was in charge.

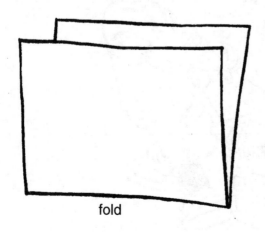

fold

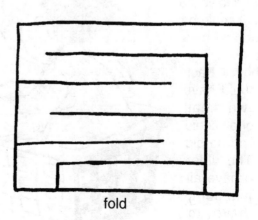

fold

Jonah: A disobedient/obedient prophet.
Pages 76-78

A DISOBEDIENT PROPHET

Text: Read and study Jonah 1:1 - 2:10.

Teaching Point: God is everywhere and we cannot run away from him.

WARM UP 1

Bring in a live goldfish in a bowl and tell the children that you are training the goldfish. Give a big build up about how well the training is going and how obedient the goldfish is. Demonstrate 'sit, roll over, stay'. Put a small hoop in for the goldfish to swim through. Toss in a small object and say 'fetch'.

Ask the children how obedient they think the goldfish is. Is the goldfish more or less disobedient than a person? Repeat some of the commands to the children, or have a leader do it all wrong (be a disobedient dog).

Today's true story from the Bible is about a fish and a person. I want you to come back and tell me:

1. What was the name of the person?

2. Which one was the most disobedient?

Note the visual aids on page 75 which can be used to retell the story of Jonah.

CONSOLIDATION 1

Races with heats and a final. The children crawl on their tummies like 'fish' to the end of the course where they eat a jelly baby (Jonah).

WIND UP 1

Get a blue sheet (or parachute) and have the children stand holding the edges. Ask them to make a rough sea and calm sea. Put a toy boat in the middle and get them to tell you the story, making the sea rough at the appropriate point. Fling a plastic figure into the middle of the sheet when Jonah is thrown overboard.

A fish can be made out of a clear plastic drinks bottle with the mouth cut out and a cardboard tail (see diagram). Show the children Jonah inside. Jonah can be sicked up.

Review the Warm Up questions about the disobedience of the fish and the man. Could Jonah run away from God?

A DISOBEDIENT PROPHET

Text: Read and study Jonah 1:1 - 2:10.

Teaching Point: God is everywhere and we cannot run away from him.

WARM UP 2

Tell the children to do what you command. Give a series of commands. Then tell the children to do the opposite of what you command, e.g. sit down (they stand), dance around (be still), be quiet (make a noise), etc.

Today's true story from the Bible is about a man who was God's prophet. I want you to listen carefully and say if you think he was an obedient or disobedient man. Did he do what God said or the opposite of what God said?

WIND UP 2

Review the questions from the Warm Up. Ask where God is? Ask where you can go where God isn't? Refer to the Consolidation. Point out the futility of Jonah running away and God's graciousness in sending the fish.

CONSOLIDATION 2

This activity can be done in small groups or class groups. Give each group some magazines, such as travel brochures, and a large piece of paper. They cut out pictures of all the places where they think God is and glue them around the edge of the paper. Towards the end the group leader encourages them to write and colour letters that say 'God is everywhere'. (Leaders will need to draw the letters for the younger children to colour.)

AN OBEDIENT PROPHET

Text: Read and study Jonah 3:1 - 4:11.

Teaching point: God has mercy on everyone who repents.

WARM UP 1

Tell last week's part of the story with deliberate and as ridiculous as possible mistakes. The children have to notice them and put them right. E.g. tell the people of Nineveh to stop going 'bong' (instead of doing wrong), God's prophet Moaner (not Jonah), swallowed by a giant spider, etc.

In today's true story from the Bible we will see what happened next. Come back and tell me:

1. What happened in Nineveh?

2. What did God do?

3. How did Jonah feel about it?

CONSOLIDATION 1

Cut out and hide worms and vine leaves. The children have to find them. One worm is special (bigger or a different colour). The children stick their vine leaves onto a long piece of string to make a vine. Hook the vine onto the wall or other handy object to act as a pulley so that the vine can grow and wilt. Retell the story with someone being Jonah and the special worm being the one to eat the vine.

WIND UP 1

Review the questions from the Warm Up. Point out that God had mercy on the Ninevites, even though they were Israel's enemies. God has mercy on anyone who repents.

WARM UP 2

Skit or puppets (see script on page 86). Trudy enters feeling very cross, because a letter she is expecting has not arrived. Toby enters, bright and cheerful, and wants to know what is the matter. Trudy turns on him and asks where all her special things are that Toby has borrowed. Toby says that he will return them tomorrow. Trudy is furious. Tomorrow is not soon enough; she wants them back now. Toby apologises, but Trudy refuses to accept it. Toby exits with Trudy following, still telling him off.

The leader comments on how sad it is that Trudy would not forgive Toby. Today's true story from the Bible is about some people who were forgiven because they were truly sorry. Come back and tell me:

1. Who were the people?

2. Who forgave them?

3. Who did not want them to be forgiven?

CONSOLIDATION 2

Jonah tag. One child is Jonah. He has one-two minutes to catch as many Ninevites (the rest of the children) as possible. When caught they sit at the sides of the room, repentant. At the end total up his score and choose another Jonah. The one who causes most to repent is the winner.

WIND UP 2

Remind the children about the Warm Up and review the questions. Was Jonah right? Refer to the game. God always has mercy on anyone who is truly repentant.

THE ENEMY DEFEATED

The leader checks if there are any visitors and asks them their names and ages.

Leader: **We have a(nother) visitor today, who's very shy. I wonder where he's hiding?**

Toby appears.

Leader: **There you are, Toby. Say hello to everyone.**

Toby: **Hello, everyone.**

Leader: **Toby's been to Sunday School before, haven't you, Toby?**

Toby: **You bet. I was here last week, matter of fact.**

Leader: **Were you? I didn't see you.**

Toby: **Well, I was here. And I listened to what was going on. All that honey and chickens and long hair. In fact, it was so good I went home and told my sister all about it. She's come with me today, but she's even more shy than what I am.**

Leader: **Where is she?**

Toby: **She's hiding back here somewhere.** [Looks down behind board.]

Come on, Trudy, you can come out. You needn't be frightened of (Leader's name) - [*looks at Leader, then at audience*] **- or the other kids.**

Trudy slowly appears.

Leader: **Hello, Trudy. I'm so glad you could come to Sunday School today.**

Trudy looks coy.

Toby: **Trudy liked hearing about last week, didn't you, Trude?**

Trudy nods.

Leader: **What was the name of the man in the Bible story last week, Trudy?**

Trudy: **Samson.**

Toby: **That's right, Trudy. And what was so special about him.**

Trudy: **He was very strong - a real he-man.**

Toby: **Yes. And what else?**

Trudy: **He had really big muscles.**

Toby: **And?**

Trudy: **He had lovely long hair. He looked real cool.**

Toby: **Yes. But there was something else special about him, Trude.**

Trudy: **Was there?**

Toby: **Yes. Why did he have long hair?**

Trudy: **Oh, you mean he was a Nazareth.**

Toby: **No, Trude, Nazareth is a place. Its where Jesus lived. Samson was a Nazirite.**

Trudy: **Oh, I remember, a Nazirite.**

Toby: **Well, what was a Nazirite?**

Trudy: **Someone with long hair?**

Toby: **Oh, sisters! A Nazirite was someone who made a promise to serve God in a special way for a period of time.**

Trudy: **But you told me Samson was a Naza-whatsit from the time he was born!**

Toby: **That's right.**

Trudy: **But how could he be? Babies can't make promises! They can't speak, they can only cry.**

Toby:	Before Samson was born an angel told his mum he was to be a Nazirite.
Trudy:	Now I remember. He couldn't drink wine.
Toby:	It wasn't only wine, Trudy. He couldn't drink any alcohol. In fact, he couldn't eat anything that came from a grapevine.
Trudy:	What, no grapes?
Toby:	[Shakes head.] No.
Trudy:	Nor raisins?
Toby:	[Shakes head.] No.
Trudy:	So he couldn't drink wine or alcohol or eat grapes or eat raisins. Is that all?
Toby:	No.
Trudy:	It's getting a bit complicated, Toby. I don't think I can remember any more.
Toby:	Perhaps (Leader's name) will help. There's some pictures on the table. Could you pin them up on the board to remind us, please?
Leader:	Of course I will.
Toby:	A Nazirite couldn't drink any wine or alcohol. *Leader pins up picture of wine goblet.*
Trudy:	And he couldn't eat grapes or raisins. *Leader pins up picture of grapes.*
Toby:	And he couldn't go near a dead body.
Trudy:	Ugh. *Leader pins up picture of a dead body.*
Trudy:	And he couldn't cut his hair! *Leader pins up picture of long hair.*
Trudy:	But, Toby?
Toby:	Yes?
Trudy:	You told me that Samson gave a big party when he got married.
Toby:	So?
Trudy:	Well, people always drank wine at weddings, didn't they? So Samson didn't keep that bit of the promise, did he?
Toby:	No. *Leader makes a cross over the wine goblet.*
Trudy:	And you told me that Samson killed a lion, then ate honey from a bees' nest in the lion's body.
Toby:	That's right. He didn't keep that bit of the promise either.
	Leader makes a cross over the dead body.
Trudy:	I don't think Samson was a very nice man. He didn't seem to care about God. Did God punish him for not keeping the promise?
Toby:	Not in the story we had last week. In fact the Bible says that God gave him his great strength.
Trudy:	I don't understand that. I always get punished when I do something wrong.
Toby:	Perhaps God didn't punish him because he didn't break all of the promise. After all, he didn't cut his hair, did he?
Trudy:	Ah, no, he didn't. Perhaps that's the reason why.

The leader sends the children off to class with appropriate questions.

The puppets remain visible until the children have gone.

DAVID KEEPS HIS PROMISES

Trudy: **Oh, hello, there. Have you seen Toby?** [Calls] **Toby! Toby! Where are you?** [Trudy waits for a response.] **Toby's never here when I want him. Will you help me call him? All together, on the count of three, call, Toby! Where are you? 1, 2, 3! Toby! Where are you?** [Pause] **That wasn't loud enough. Come on, 1 ,2, 3. Toby! Where are you?**

Enter Toby.

Toby: **What's all that noise? Oh, it's you, Trudy. I might have known - your voice is like a foghorn, all loud and croaky.**

Trudy: **Don't be so rude. It was the boys and girls calling as well.**

Toby: **OK, so their voices are like foghorns too.**

Trudy: **You are awful, Toby. Anyway, I wanted to see you. 'Cos I've got lots to tell you, that's why. I've been doing lots and lots of exciting things.**

Toby: **Such as?**

Trudy: **I've been to school, I played skipping, I've done all my homework and ....**

Toby: **That sounds really exciting, Trudy.** [To the children] **Boy, if that's her idea of excitement, you can keep it. I'd get more excitement from watching milk boil!**

Trudy: **So, what have you been up to? I bet you haven't done anything special.**

Toby: **Well, that's where you're wrong. I played football every night this week. And I scored some goals for my team. And we won. So there.**

Trudy: **Football. That's all you think about, Toby. I think football's a stupid game.**

Toby: **You just don't understand it. Anyway, let's not argue. What are you doing this week?**

Trudy: **Oh, I'm really excited about this week. And especially about going to the cinema.**

Toby: **Going to the cinema, are you?**

Trudy: **Of course I am. We're going to see (name of current children's film).**

Toby: **What do you mean, we're going to see it?**

Trudy: **On Tuesday. We're going to see (name of film). You know we are. You promised.**

Toby: **When did I promise? I don't remember promising to go to the cinema.**

Trudy: **Yes you did. Three weeks ago. I was saying how much I wanted to see (name of film), and you said we would go and see it when it came to our cinema.**

Toby: **Well, I didn't know it was coming this week.**

Trudy: **But I told you. Last week. And you said Tuesday was OK. You did, Toby.**

Toby: **I don't remember saying Tuesday was OK. I can't have been listening.**

Trudy: **Toby, you promised.**

Toby: **I may have promised, but I didn't mean now. How about next month, or next year?**

Trudy: **The film won't be on next month. You are mean, Toby. You promised we'd go.**

Toby: **Well, Tuesday's no good.**

Trudy: **Why not? Why won't you keep your promise, Toby?**

Toby: **My friend, George, has invited me to go with him to a football match. And that is far more important than going to a silly old film.**

Trudy: **But I thought you were my friend.**

Toby: **Yes, I am. But I'm George's friend as well, and he asked me this morning to go with him and I said yes. So, I've got to go. I've promised.**

Trudy: **You promised me we'd go to the film.**

Toby: **Well, it's not convenient at the moment.** [Trudy looks sad.] **Don't get upset, Trudy. We'll go to the cinema one day. I just can't say which one. Anyway, I've got to go now. I've promised to meet George to play football. Bye.**

Toby leaves, leaving Trudy looking droopy.

ELIJAH AND THE DROUGHT

Trudy: Hello, girls and boys. We're at summer camp again. Have you seen my brother Toby? I wonder where that boy is? I bet he's getting into all sorts of mischief, and being really naughty. Toby! Toby! Where are you? There's some people to meet you.

Toby: Where, where? [*Looks round.*] Oh, hello boys and girls. Good to meet you all. Toby's the name, and getting up to mischief is my game! Ha ha! [*Turns to Trudy*] What have you been doing, Trudy?

Trudy: I've been racing around the grounds with all my friends.

Toby: Racing round the grounds? You don't race - you just amble.

Trudy: We don't just amble. We run. And we have fun.

Toby: Bet you don't have as much fun as we do!

Trudy: Yes, we do!

Toby: OK. What did you do yesterday?

Trudy: Well, after my friend Rachel arrived we went to all our favourite places.

Toby: Yuk! [*Pretends to puke.*]

Trudy: And then we built a den, just like last year.

Toby: Did you build it in the same place?

Trudy: I'm not telling you.

Toby: Oh, go on, Trudy, be a sport.

Trudy: No!

Toby: Please tell me.

Trudy: No!

Toby: Why not?

Trudy: 'Cos last year you and your friends mucked it up.

Toby: [*Innocently*] Did we? I don't remember mucking up any old den.

Trudy: Yes you did! You and Percy waited 'til we'd gone swimming in the lake and you mucked it up. When we got back it was all broken and spoilt.

Toby: You don't know it was us, Trudy. After all, you and Rachel weren't even there.

Trudy: How do you know that unless you did it?

Toby: 'Cos you just said so, stupid.

[*Singing from offstage.*]

Toby: Oh, here's Percy coming.

[*Max enters.*]

Toby: Hi, Percy. Good to see you again.

Max: Hello, Toby. Isn't it a great day? Isn't it good to be here again?

Trudy: Percy, have you seen Rachel anywhere? We arranged to meet here 10 minutes ago.

Max: Uh, Rachel?

[*Noise from off stage. Percy enters.*]

Trudy: Percy? But Percy's already here. [*Looks round.*]

Toby: Hang on - what's happening here? Am I seeing double, or am I seeing double? [*To Percy*] Who are you?

Percy: Don't be silly, Toby, I'm Percy.

Max: No he isn't! I'm Percy.

Percy: But I'm Percy.

Toby: OK you two, stop messing around. Which one of you is Percy?

Max:	I'm Percy.
Percy:	No, I'm Percy.
Max:	I'm Percy.
Percy:	I'm Percy.
Toby:	Shut up, both of you! Trudy, which one of these 2 idiots is Percy?
Trudy:	I don't know. Ask that one [*pointing at Max*].
Toby:	[*Exasperatedly*] I've already asked him, clothhead, and all he says is he's Percy.
Trudy:	Well, there's no need to shout at me, just 'cos you don't know either. Why not ask the boys and girls?
Toby:	So you do have a brain after all. Boys and girls, can you help? Which one of these 2 is Percy?
	Is this one Percy? [*Max looks round grinning.*] Or is this one Percy? [*Percy looks round grinning.*] Well you weren't much help.
Trudy:	Does it really matter if we know who the real Percy is?
Toby:	Of course it matters! Percy's my friend. We do things together. We talk together. I listen to what he has to say.
Trudy:	Well you'll just have to work out a way of telling them apart, won't you?
Max:	Don't worry your head over that, Toby. You can believe me. I'm Percy.
Percy:	No you're not. I'm Percy. [*The puppets tussle.*]
Trudy:	Stop fighting you two! It's not nice to fight. [*Puppets stop fighting.*]
Percy:	I'm the real Percy.
Max:	No you're not. I'm the real Percy.
Toby:	Stop it, you two. I know what I'll do. I'll give you a test.
Max:	A test?
Percy:	A test? That's a good idea.
Trudy:	What sort of test?
Toby:	Well, you know I said that Percy and I did things together and talked together?
Trudy:	Yes.
Toby:	And you know we were talking earlier about your den, Trudy?
Trudy:	Yes.
Toby:	I have a confession to make. It was Percy and me who ruined it for you.
Trudy:	I knew that already.
Toby:	So, if it was Percy and me wot ruined your den, only Percy and me'll know exactly how we did it, won't we?
Trudy:	Yes.
Toby:	OK, Percy, [*looking at Max*] what did we do first?
Max:	You can't expect me to remember every detail of what we did a year ago, Toby?
Percy:	But I remember, 'cos I'm the real Percy. We waited 'til Trudy and Rachel went swimming. Then we crept through the bushes to make sure no one saw us. Then we knocked down the walls of the den and scattered the branches, didn't we, Toby?
Toby:	That's exactly what we did! Now we all know who the real Percy is.
Trudy:	That's right. The real Percy is the one whose words were true. [*To Max*] So, who are you?
Max:	I'm Percy's cousin, Max.
Trudy:	You are clever, Toby.
Toby	Oh, it was nothing really. We boys just know what to do, that's all. Let's go and build a new den, everyone.

JOB

Enter Toby.

Toby: **Hello, boys and girls. How are you today?** [*Waits for a response.*]

Oh, I've had such a terrible, terrible time lately. Everything's gone wrong. First the goldfish died. Oh, dear. [*Toby sighs.*] **I'd just sorted that out when I got my finger shut in the door.** [*Sighs*] **So I got that bandaged and I found I'd lost my homework. I looked everywhere, but it was nowhere to be found. I'm going to get into such trouble at school. Oh, dear. And do you know what else happened? The cat was sick in my bed. It's too much.**

Enter Trudy, singing.

Trudy: **Hello girls and boys, it's nice to see you again. I'm having such a good day. Oh, hello Toby, how are you?**

Toby: **I'm not good. I'm having a terrible time.**

Trudy: **What's the matter?**

Toby: **Everything's gone wrong. First the goldfish died. Oh, dear.** [*Toby sighs.*] **I'd just sorted that out when I got my finger shut in the door.** [*Sighs*] **So I got that bandaged and I found I'd lost my homework. I looked everywhere, but it was nowhere to be found. I'm going to get into such trouble at school. Oh, dear. And do you know what else happened? The cat was sick in my bed. It's too much.**

Trudy: **But that's terrible. You poor thing.**

Toby: **I don't understand why all this has happened. And why has it happened to me?**

Trudy: [*Pause for thought*] **Perhaps you got out of bed on the wrong side?**

Toby: **I can't have, my bed's against a wall.**

Trudy: **Umm, perhaps you broke a mirror, or walked under a ladder? My gran says that's seven years bad luck.**

Toby: **No, I don't believe all that stuff. It's just rubbish.**

Trudy: **Or maybe a black cat did something, I forget what?**

Toby: **No, there's got to be some proper reason why these things have happened.**

Trudy: **I don't know. You're probably just having a bad day.**

Toby: **Perhaps God is punishing me for being naughty.**

Trudy: **Don't be daft. You're always being naughty, and nothing like this has happened before - has it?**

Toby: **No. You're right.** [*Pause, while both puppets think.*]

Toby: **Perhaps God just doesn't love me any more.**

Trudy: **Don't be silly, of course he does. He always loves us.**

Toby: **But I'm not a good boy sometimes.**

Trudy: **God doesn't love you 'cos you're good. And he doesn't stop loving you when you've been bad.**

Toby: **Thank you, Trudy. I feel better now.** [*Pause*] **But I've still had a terrible day.**

UNDECIDED ABOUT GOD'S WORD

Puppets Toby and Trudy giving conflicting advice about 3 or 4 different coloured buckets on a table. In a hat somewhere in the room is a soft toy. The leader introduces Toby and Trudy.

Leader: [*looking around*] **I've lost my (soft toy).** [*Describe the soft toy.*] **Has anyone seen it?**

Trudy: **It's under a bucket!**

Toby: **No, it isn't!**

Trudy: **Yes, it is. It's under the red one!**

Leader: [*to audience*] **Whom should I believe, Toby or Trudy?**
Wait for audience response.

Toby: **It can't be under the red bucket, because it's too small.**

Trudy: **It is under the red bucket!**

Toby: **It's not under the red bucket. It's in the (black) hat!**

Leader: [*to audience*] **Whom should I believe?** [*Take a vote.*]
Let's look under the red bucket! [*look under bucket.*]

Trudy: **Sorry, I made a mistake. It's under the white bucket.**

Leader: **Are you sure?**

Toby: [*bouncing up and down*] **It's in the hat!**

Trudy: **It can't be in the hat. It's too small and it doesn't wear a hat anyway!**

Leader: **Let's take a look under the white bucket!** [*look under bucket.*]

Toby: **I told you so. Look in the hat!**

Trudy: **Sorry, my mistake. It's under the grey bucket. I know because it has a label on it. I promise it's there. Really, really, really!**

Leader: [*asks audience*] **Should I believe Trudy's promise?**

Trudy: **If it's not under the grey bucket you can have this block of chocolate.**

Leader: **OK. That sounds reasonable.** [*look under bucket. Takes the chocolate only to discover that there is no chocolate in the packaging.*]

Leader: **I think I've been listening to the wrong person.** [*Turns to Toby.*]

Toby: **I keep telling you, it's in the hat.**

The leader picks up the hat and produces the soft toy.

AN OBEDIENT PROPHET

Trudy enters feeling very cross.

Trudy: [*shouting and raging*] **It's not good enough!** [*sees the children*] **Oh, hello. I'm sorry I was shouting, but I'm really fed up. The second post has been and my letter** still **hasn't arrived. They promised it would be here today. Oooh, if only I had them here, I'd show them!**

Toby appears, bright and confident.

Toby: **You'd show them what?**

Trudy: **Listen, cloth ears, it's nothing to do with you.**

Toby: [*remaining calm*] **What's wrong, Trudy? Why all the fuss?**

Trudy: **You shouldn't be listening to other people's conversations. Go away. I don't want you.**

Toby: **My uncle Sigmund always said that it's healthy to express our most secret thoughts and emotions and not bottle them up. But in your case, Trudy, he would call you a 100% pure, unadulterated, solid gold nut!**

Trudy: [*loud and threatening*] **How dare you speak to me like that! Just you wait 'til I get my hands on you; I'll show you!**

Toby: **Hey, you've got no right to threaten me. What have I done?**

Trudy: [*threateningly*] **You, you've done more than enough!**

Toby: **Busy, aren't I?** [*mouth open in a big laugh*]

Trudy: **Busy is right. Busy borrowing my favourite (Spice Girls) records, my (Spice Girls) foot massager, my (Spice Girls) book of famous sayings, my (Spice Girls) backpack, and my (Spice Girls) reusable cereal shapes.**

Toby: **So that's what this is all about, me borrowing your special things. I'll return them tomorrow.**

Trudy: **Tomorrow's not good enough. I want them now!**

Toby: **Look, I'm sorry I didn't ask you. I won't do it again.**

Trudy: **You insect! You worm! You can't get out of this. You're dead meat, Toby!**

Toby: **Look, I've said I'm really sorry and I will return everything. Can't you forgive me?**

Trudy: **No way! I'll never forgive you for this. You've ruined my life.**

Toby: **Is there no mercy, compassion, kindness, forgiveness?**

Trudy: **I'm not in the forgiveness business, Toby. So get lost.**

Toby exits with head hanging down, closely followed by Trudy continuing to tell him off.

Contents (in Bible Order)

Contents (in OTW for 3-9s order)

Subject Index

Notes Notes Notes

Notes Notes Notes

Children can and should be taught from the very earliest age about the God who made them and loves them. For this purpose TnT Ministries have developed a comprehensive range of teaching materials. As well as explaining the fundamental truths of the Christian message this material has been specifically designed for every age group from toddlers to teenagers. There are stories, activities and craft ideas as well as lesson plans and Bible study notes to help teachers understand the scripture passages. Teachers and children will enjoy learning more about God through his word.

TnT materials are thoroughly tested by churches and teachers around the world. They are intelligible, biblically accurate and help to make teaching children enjoyable.

Pre-school: Three books - Beginning with the Bible First Class; Beginning with the Bible Old Testament; Beginning with the Bible New Testament.

3-9's: Fourteen books covering all the major doctrines of the Christian faith.

9-11's: Six books giving children a solid introduction to Bible study.

11-14's Six books to challenge and stimulate teenagers to study the Bible for themselves.

The Game is Up Old Testament Book 1 and Book 2 and soon to come: The Game is Up New Testament Book 3 and Book 4.

Do you have both books in this series?
The Game is Up
OLD TESTAMENT
Book 1 and Book 2

Book 1: Genesis, Exodus, Numbers, Joshua.
Book 2: Judges, Ruth, 1 & 2 Samuel, 1 & 2 Kings, 2 Chronicles, Nehemiah, Esther, Job, Jeremiah, Daniel, Jonah.

Take the Bible seriously and have loads of fun while you are at it!

Are you looking to add another dimension to your teaching? Do you want to encourage your children to read the Bible? Do you want them to have strong Biblical foundations without compromising on fun and activity? TnT have developed The Game Is Up for this very purpose. There is a companion volume to this book: The Game is Up Old Testament Book 1 which covers Genesis, Exodus, Numbers and Joshua. There are also plans for books on the New Testament to come out in the following year.

All the games are directly linked to the lessons with strong Biblical emphasis that covers all major Christian doctrines. Visual aids for photocopying and clearly explained teaching points make this an excellent addition to any church resource library. Book One covers Genesis, Exodus, Numbers and Joshua. Book 2 covers Judges, Ruth, 1 & 2 Samuel, 1 & 2 Kings, 2 Chronicles, Nehemiah, Esther, Job, Jeremiah, Daniel, Jonah.

☺ The successful On the Way series continued with extra games and activities.
☺ Book 1: 80 game selections;
☺ Book 2: 96 game selections
☺ Flexible enough to be used with any curriculum
☺ Strong Biblical Emphasis
☺ Multi age (3-11s)
☺ Ideal for Holiday Bible Club; Vacation Bible School

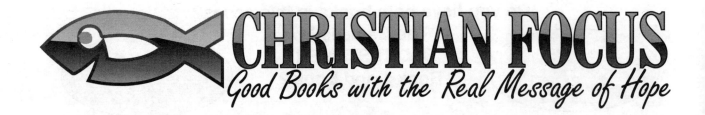

CHRISTIAN FOCUS
Good Books with the Real Message of Hope

Christian Focus Publications publishes biblically-accurate books for adults and children.

If you are looking for quality Bible teaching for children then we have a wide and excellent range of Bible story books - from board books to teenage fiction, we have it covered.

You can also try our new Bible teaching Syllabus for 3-9 year olds and teaching materials for pre-school children.

These children's books are bright, fun and full of biblical truth, an ideal way to help children discover Jesus Christ for themselves. Our aim is to help children find out about God and get them enthusiastic about reading the Bible, now and later in their lives.

Find us at our web page: www.christianfocus.com

TnT

TnT Ministries (which stands for Teaching and Training Ministries) was launched in February 1993 by Christians from a broad variety of denominational backgrounds who are concerned that teaching the Bible to children be taken seriously. The leaders were in charge of a Sunday School of 50 teachers ar St Helen's Bishopgate, an evangelical church in the city of London, for 13 years, during which time a range of Biblical teaching material has been developed. TnT Ministries also runs training days for Sunday School teachers.